Wisdom from Women in Scripture

Edited by Kelly M. Wahlquist

Teresa Tomeo ✝ Elizabeth M. Kelly ✝ Mary Healy

Melissa Overmyer ✝ Alyssa Bormes

the WORD
among us®
Press

Published by The Word Among Us Press

7115 Guilford Drive, Suite 100
Frederick, Maryland 21704

wau.org

27 26 25 24 23   1 2 3 4 5

ISBN: 978-1-59325-717-0

eISBN: 978-1-59325-718-7

Design by Rose Audette

Made and printed in the United States of America

Library of Congress Control Number: 2023920118

CONTENTS

INTRODUCTION

Open Wide the Door to Wisdom

KELLY M. WAHLQUIST

When my oldest was in first grade, she and her friends put on a skit. It was nothing elaborate. There was no grand theater, no stage, no ticket sales. There was nothing impressive about the invitation, either. "You can come down now!" one of the girls yelled to the moms upstairs, who were chatting and chewing while the kids were in the basement.

I can't remember the entire skit, but I remember the sing-songy way it began: "Sophia, Sophia . . . open the door." But nothing happens. So the three little four-footers, donned in blankets as costumes, repeat the request: "Sophia, Sophia . . . open the door!" Again, nothing happens. A third time, they make the musical request; and this time, one of the girls mysteriously appears (from underneath a blanket) as Sophia and opens wide the door. The girls chuckle as they watch the moms lovingly appear amazed. With some of the best acting of the day, one mom asks, "Where did Sophia come from?!" The littlest one replies with uncontrollable laughter, "She was here the whole time!" And joy breaks out in the basement theater.

The Greek word for "wisdom" is *sophia*—though it would be a few years before the first-grade actresses would learn that little bit of knowledge. In both Greek and Hebrew, the word for "wisdom" is a grammatically feminine noun—again, something the three young ladies would learn much later in their studies. Sophia, or Wisdom, is often personified in Scripture as a female character—an expression of the feminine aspects of God. Many theologians have followed suit. Throughout his book *Emblems of a Season of Fury*, Thomas Merton refers to Sophia grammatically in the feminine.

> Sophia is Gift, is Spirit, *Donum Dei*. She is God-given and God Himself as Gift. Sophia in all things is the Divine Life reflected in them. . . . Sophia is God sharing of Himself with creatures, His outpouring, and the Love by which He is given and known, held and loved. She is in all things like the air receiving the sunlight.[1]

In the Book of Wisdom, Sophia guides the Exodus people through the wilderness: "She guided them along a marvelous way, and became a shelter to them by day, and a starry flame through the night" (10:17). In the same way, in *Wisdom from Women in Scripture*, I firmly believe Sophia was guiding the writers such that, in their words, you will find shelter in the wilderness of your life and direction in the darkness.

WISDOM FROM WOMEN IN THE SCRIPTURES

It has been a tremendous blessing for me to write this book with five amazing Catholic women! Each has a deep love of

Sacred Scripture and is a leader and evangelizer in her own right. Every writer prayerfully chose a female biblical character she connected to in some way. The individual chapters beautifully articulate the author's perspective, thought, or experience. I hope you will be moved and inspired by the lives of these saints and the stories that will connect you to them.

You will journey into the heart of a relationship with Ruth, who leaves her home to care for another. In Ruth, Naomi has found a loving and trusted young friend—one ready to take risks and to act boldly and decisively for the good of them both. In Naomi, Ruth has found a wise and compassionate mature voice to guide her, leading to something much greater than either of them could imagine.

Esther is the queen who dared to see her position as an opportunity to save the lives of a whole nation. She had a place of influence, providing a powerful example of how God can use each of us. Esther trusted God's direction, preparing physically and spiritually for the imminent responsibility she was being called to.

The woman with the alabaster jar pushed past fear and condemning eyes to worship Jesus. Seeing and responding with her heart, she personifies the gift of sensitivity. Her gift shows us what it means to give a radical, total gift of self, without counting the cost, in response to Jesus' total gift of himself to us.

The woman at the well demonstrates what it means to be a disciple of Jesus, equipped with the joy and zeal necessary to engage in the new evangelization. She is a model for all women who have encountered Jesus. She teaches us to be open and receptive to a relationship with the Lord, to be sensitive to him and engage him with our heart and mind, to embrace the love of the Lord and generously share it.

Rahab surrenders to Jesus as he saves her from the very real disorder of her life and the chaos of her Jericho walls. Her story teaches us how the Holy Spirit hovers over our chaos, healing, bringing order, and the promise of new life in Christ.

At the Annunciation, Mary is becoming exactly who she is meant to be, who she has been created to be—the mother of God. Uttering her *fiat* (her "yes") must have brought her the greatest joy and fulfillment she could have known. That is the work of the Holy Spirit, to help us to know the deepest desires of our heart, given to us by the Father, and to help us become who we are meant to be in his kingdom.

Each of these women in the Scriptures responds with a resounding "Yes!" to the call of God. They are discerning and surrendered as they step into the unknown of God's plan for them. The Church, too, is historically filled with courageous women like this—women who, in the most challenging times, have a healthy sense of self that frees them to serve without improperly losing themselves. They recognize their own humanity and their own uniqueness as created by God, and in doing so, these saints pass their wisdom on for generations to come.

Much like in the skit of the seven-year-olds in a basement long ago, Sophia (or the Wisdom of God) has always been with us throughout the generations.

In the first chapter of John, what the author says about "the Word of God" was said about Sophia in the Jewish tradition. Like the Word, Sophia was present with God before creation. Just as the Word was with God and was God, so Sophia was.[2]

Sophia has been with us since the beginning. Though we may not see her under the blankets of shame and unworthiness or whatever we have tossed on her throughout our lives, she is there and longing for us to reveal and embrace her.

As you read *Wisdom from Women in Scripture*, I pray you will recognize God's plan for your life and be encouraged to embrace your gifts to build his kingdom. May your eyes be opened to the God who sees you, loves you, and brings you healing, courage, and mercy right where you are, and may you boldly knock and ask Sophia to open wide the door of your heart, so you may see as God sees.

A woman came with an alabaster jar of ointment of pure nard, very costly, and she broke the jar and poured it over his head. (Mark 14:3)

1.

A Simple Gesture of Love

The Woman with the Alabaster Jar

The moment Ani Pennings saw the photo of three-year-old Pepito on her adoption agency's listing, she knew it in her heart: *This is our son.* She showed the photo to her husband, Jeff, who agreed, "Yes, that's our son." Pepito's face, though peaceful, already bore traces of the illnesses he had endured. He was born in a remote area of Ethiopia, and from his birth he suffered from hydrocephalus, which went untreated for eighteen months, leading to epilepsy, cerebral palsy, blindness, and a diagnosis list a mile long.

Ani and Jeff knew that caring for Pepito would mean suffering. They began to prepare and ask the Lord to give them the grace to suffer. They also knew that Pepito's time on earth would be limited and that no matter how much time the Lord gave them with him, it would never feel like enough. From the moment they chose to adopt him, they decided that they just wanted to love Pepito and enjoy every moment for as long as they had him.

Suffering did indeed come. From the day they met Pepito in Ethiopia in 2015, they watched him experience muscle spasms and seizures. After they brought him home to Michigan, Ani cared for him through many surgery recoveries, spent weeks by his side in the hospital as he suffered through pancreatitis, and sat up with him countless nights on the couch, holding him so he could breathe comfortably when he had a virus.

That is not to say Pepito's life was all suffering. He loved his parents and three siblings and enjoyed all the little events of daily life with them—basketball, soccer, school Masses, even stadium cleanup after a football game. He went camping with them all over Michigan, road-tripping to Boston and Maine, and traveling to Mexico.

Pepito was with his family for eight short years. At his funeral, Ani described what life was like with Pepito:

> In our home Pepito was constantly being cuddled and kissed. His older brother was thrilled to have another boy in the family so the two of them could share a room. His older sister would stroke his head and sing made-up songs to him. The two of them have grown up to be the sweetest, most sensitive older siblings, learning and taking on more and more of his care, with so much love for their younger brother. His little sister (also with special needs) showered Pepito with

as much love and affection as she possibly could. We gave him all the love that we could and enjoyed every moment that we had.

In the eyes of many people, Pepito's life would be considered a waste. He completed no education, won no prizes, made no notable contributions in any field of human endeavor, and was incapable of serving or providing for others. Because of his inability to speak and see, most normal forms of human interaction were out of bounds for him. The enormous investment that his parents made in him would also be considered by many to be a waste. Why not spend their energies on a child with a better prognosis, or someone who would at least grow to adulthood and enjoy a full life?

Yet in the eyes of the Lord, Pepito's life was unimaginably precious. It held a value that could not be measured by any human calculations, in comparison with which all the gold and silver in the world is gray dust. Not one ounce of the love, time, attention, or expense lavished on him by his family was a waste. There is a treasure beyond price that is invisible to the calculating eyes of the world. And it can only be found by giving all that one has without counting the cost.

A Memorable Dinner Party

There is a woman in the Gospels who understood this. She is not a prominent figure, nor is she, as far as we know, one of the holy women present at Jesus' cross and empty tomb. She is mentioned in only a single episode. In all but one of the

Gospel accounts, she is not even named; she is known only as the woman with the alabaster jar. Yet her one recorded interaction with Jesus is so full of significance that Jesus himself made it an inseparable part of the proclamation of his good news until the end of history:

"Amen, I say to you, wherever the gospel is preached in the whole world, what she has done will be told in memory of her."
(Mark 14:9)

From the time I came to know the Lord myself, I have been deeply moved by the story of this woman, whose simple gesture of love is a model for disciples of Jesus. The episode is told in three (or possibly all four) of the Gospels, but here I will unfold the story focusing mainly on the version according to St. Mark (Mark 14:3-9).[3]

And while he was at Bethany in the house of Simon the leper, as he sat at table, a woman came with an alabaster jar of ointment of pure nard, very costly, and she broke the jar and poured it over his head. (Mark 14:3)

The Gospel is sparing in the details, but we can imagine the scene. Jesus, the honored rabbi from Nazareth, has been invited to a formal dinner party along with his disciples. "Simon the leper" may have been among those healed by Jesus. In fact, he must have been healed in some way since no one would have come to dine at the home of a ritually unclean person carrying a deadly contagious disease. Simon no doubt went all out to lay a feast before his eminent guest, using his best pottery and linens and perhaps "killing the fatted calf" (see Luke 15:27). At mealtimes in the biblical world, people would recline on mats on the floor, in a semicircle, with the food in bowls or platters on a low table in the middle.

In the midst of the festivities, suddenly an uninvited person walks in. She is carrying an alabaster flask of pure nard, an aromatic oil made from a root native to India. We later find out that the nard is breathtakingly expensive, worth a year's wages—in our terms, tens of thousands of dollars. Such an item would be a treasured heirloom, possibly even her dowry lovingly set aside for the day of her wedding. The only other place where nard appears in the Bible is in the Song of Songs, as one of the fragrances of the bride that enchants the bridegroom.

The presence of nard gives a nuptial air to the whole scene. For those with eyes to see (or noses to scent), the honored guest at table is none other than the divine Bridegroom. And this is no ordinary meal but the messianic wedding feast promised by God through the prophets (see Isaiah 25:6; 55:1-2; Song of Songs 2:3; 5:1).

But the dinner guests are oblivious to the true significance of the occasion. As they look on in stunned indignation, the woman breaks (literally, *shatters*) the flask and pours it on the head of Jesus. In that society, as in ours, such a disruption by an uninvited person would be at best awkward, and likely a serious embarrassment to the host. But this woman is clearly unconcerned about decorum or the reaction of other people. Her gaze is fixed on Jesus alone. The fact that she shatters the flask means that she keeps not even one drop for herself. She is not counting the cost.

Who was this woman, and what did she mean? The Gospel gives us few clues, but we can surmise that she had already encountered Jesus at some point. She must have had a profound experience of healing or forgiveness or unconditional love from him, and she wanted to express her love in return. To pour fragrant oil on a person's head was a gracious gesture of hospitality (see Psalm 23:5; 133:2; Luke 7:46). So when she found out that Jesus was at table in the home of Simon the leper, she took her chance. It was her way of showing extravagant love, of giving Jesus the very best she had.

WHY THIS WASTE?

But for readers familiar with the Old Testament, there is a deeper significance. In ancient Israel, kings were installed in office not by being crowned (as in European history), but by being *anointed* with oil perfumed with costly spices (see 1 Samuel 10:1; 16:13). This is why the king was called the Lord's "anointed" (1 Samuel 24:10) or messiah (Hebrew *mashiah*; the Greek equivalent is *christos*, Christ). The marvelous fragrance the oil left behind was like an invisible crown, conferring an aura of holiness, so that the king was recognized as belonging to God in a unique way. The psalmist celebrates this anointing when he extols the king:

God, your God, has anointed you with the oil of gladness above your fellows; your robes are all fragrant with myrrh and aloes and cassia. (Psalm 45:7-8)

Not only kings but priests, too, were ordained to their sacred office by being anointed with sacred oil (see Exodus 29:7).

For many centuries the Jews had hoped, prayed, and longed for the coming of the Messiah, the anointed king promised by God. And this woman, by pouring out her nard on the head of Jesus, is proclaiming that *Jesus* is the hoped-for Messiah. Remarkably, it is the only time in his earthly life that Jesus is literally anointed, and it is just days before he accomplishes his messianic mission by dying and rising from the dead. Indeed, it is likely that the scent of the ointment with which she anointed him—the fragrance of royalty—lingered on Jesus during the final days of his life. While he was on trial, mocked, scourged, stripped naked, and nailed to the cross, he exuded the aroma of a king.

Was this woman aware of the full significance of her gesture? Probably not. If she was, her bravery is even more evident, since such a royal anointing was an act with political repercussions. Any attempt to establish what appeared to be a rival kingship would be regarded as sedition by the Romans (see Mark 15:2), and would be punished accordingly.[4]

Jesus' disciples and the other dinner guests, however, are not impressed.[5] On the contrary, they are incensed.

> But there were some who said to themselves indignantly, "Why was the ointment thus wasted? For this ointment might have been sold for more than three hundred denarii, and given to the poor." And they reproached her.
>
> (Mark 14:4-5)

Why this waste? At first glance, their objection may seem reasonable. The ointment would have generated an enormous revenue that could have been donated to the poor. Jesus, in continuity with the Old Testament Scriptures, had taught the importance of generosity to the poor (see Mark 10:21; Luke 12:33; 14:13). For the Jews, it was customary to give charitable donations on feast days in particular, and the feast of Passover was near. That is why when Judas left the last supper, the other disciples assumed he was going to carry out that very duty (John 13:29).

But "waste" means giving pointlessly, giving more than is due. If a nickel will do and you give a dollar, it's a waste. If two days are enough for a job and you spend five days on it, it's a waste. To be wasteful is to give too much for too little in return.[6] *But can anything given to Jesus be a waste?* No, it is impossible to spend too much on him! Whoever thinks something can be wasted on Jesus simply does not know who he is, or perhaps has never had their heart captivated by the divine Bridegroom, the fulfillment of all desire.

So infuriated were the guests at the woman's destruction of a valuable financial resource that they "reproached her," or literally, *snorted at her*—the same verb used for the snorting of a horse. Their reaction only shows their obliviousness to what is happening. They were in favor of programs, projects, and social action with measurable results. But this woman recognized the primacy of love. She bore witness that Jesus is worthy of ALL, of her whole life being poured out. Charitable donations are secondary. That which is first and best belongs to the Bridegroom himself—the one who will be soon "taken away" by his passion (Mark 2:20). By her extravagant gesture, this woman proclaimed louder than words that nothing is too good for Jesus.

The Gospel of John adds a poignant detail:

The house was filled with the fragrance of the ointment.
(John 12:3)

Wherever the Gospel mentions a house, it is speaking on a symbolic level of the Church, the house of God. When she broke that flask, pouring out the nard on Jesus, everyone in the house became aware of the sweetest, most beguiling fragrance. That odor of Bethany still fills the Church today.[7] Whenever a person pours out on Jesus what is most valuable, loving him to folly without counting the cost, it bears witness that he is worthy of our all. The fragrance of his presence wafts out to the Church, and even to the wider community. As Paul exclaims,

Thanks be to God, who in Christ always leads us in triumph, and through us spreads the fragrance of the knowledge of him everywhere. For we are the aroma of Christ to God

among those who are being saved and among those who
are perishing. (2 Corinthians 2:14-15)

A Beautiful Thing

Whether or not the woman fully recognized the significance
of her act, Jesus did. And he was deeply moved. Up to now,
the Gospel has shown Jesus continuously ministering to people:
healing, feeding, forgiving, delivering from demons. Only the
angels, Peter's mother-in-law, and the faithful women who
accompanied Jesus have ministered to *him*.[8] Now, as he is about
to undergo his passion, once again a woman is ministering to
him. Jesus reproaches those who had rebuked her,

"Let her alone; why do you trouble her? She has done a
beautiful thing to me. For you always have the poor with
you, and whenever you will, you can do good to them; but
you will not always have me. She has done what she could;
she has taken my body beforehand to anoint it for burial."
(Mark 14:6-8, literal translation)

Jesus' response to the critics is a permanent encouragement to all those who do as she did: Don't listen to those who
say, *Why this waste!* Don't worry about what the world thinks.
Don't even be troubled by the misunderstanding of some in the
Church, who advise you against such a "waste."

She has done a beautiful thing for the King of kings himself,
an act of love he will never forget. A "beautiful thing" is a biblical

term for an act of charity or almsgiving.[9] By speaking of her gesture as a "beautiful thing" done to him, Jesus places himself in the position of a beggar, the recipient of an act of charity.

Jesus then refers to a passage in the law of Moses:

"The poor will never cease out of the land; therefore I command you, You shall open wide your hand to your brother, to the needy and to the poor, in the land." (Deuteronomy 15:11)

The fact that poverty persists, despite all the attempts throughout history to eliminate it, is no excuse to ignore the plight of the poor. Rather it is a constant reminder of our obligation to care for them. Jesus himself identifies with the hungry, the naked, the alien, and the sick, and will declare at the end of time,

"As you did it to one of the least of these my brethren, you did it to me." (Matthew 25:40)

So it is not that the disciples were wrong to be concerned about donations to the poor.

But here is what they missed:

"You will not always have me." (Mark 14:7)

It is a veiled prophecy of Jesus' passion, which was soon to begin. The woman has done what she could, emptying her flask on the One who was about to empty himself for us. Whereas the disciples were moderate, balanced, and measured in their response to Jesus, the woman was reckless. She held nothing back, like the poor widow who put her two last coins into the temple treasury, losing her chance of even getting a hunk of bread for dinner. She poured out on the Lord what was most precious to her, even to the point of apparent waste.

Jesus then makes a curious statement that can be translated literally:

"She has taken my body beforehand to anoint it for burial."
(Mark 14:8, literal translation)

Her action, he is saying, was a prophecy in gesture. Somehow, intuitively, she foresaw his passion and prepared his body with the traditional Jewish anointing of the deceased. In fact, the passion account ends with other women going to the tomb to anoint Jesus for burial (see Mark 16:1). But their mission is not accomplished, because he is risen! Only this woman succeeds, because she anointed him *beforehand*.

On a deeper level, she prepared Jesus for his death by affirming the unspeakable value of the life he was about to pour out. By lavishing on him what was most precious, she gave her "yes" to his passion. The disciples, in contrast, had rejected the passion. In fact, when Jesus first foretold his sufferings, Peter had urged him not to go to the cross (see Mark 8:32). Why? Precisely because, according to human calculations, it seemed a waste. Jesus was doing so many good things—performing miracles, giving wise teachings, attracting crowds. Soon he would ride into Jerusalem and be acclaimed king. To speak of rejection, torture, and an agonizing death seemed a complete waste of the whole project.

But this woman assents to the passion by symbolically anticipating what Jesus himself will do: pour out his whole life, recklessly, for us. She is therefore the first person in the Gospel to truly understand the meaning of the cross. Her gesture is the human "yes" Jesus sought before going through with his sufferings. It is the bridal response to his spousal gift of himself. So he concludes by saying,

"Amen, I say to you, wherever the gospel is preached in the whole world, what she has done will be told in memory of her."
(Mark 14:9)

It is a solemn pledge: her gesture will always be remembered and coupled with what he himself did. Her act, exemplifying the right response to Jesus' passion, will "be told" as an essential part of the proclamation of gospel. And indeed it is, to this day. The preaching of the good news of Christ will lead countless others to do what she did: to waste themselves on him.

There is a further hidden significance to her gesture that the Evangelist subtly demonstrates with a series of striking parallels. Soon after the anointing at Bethany, there is another ritual action, again in the context of table fellowship, that symbolically anticipates Jesus' passion: the institution of the Eucharist.

The two episodes are like mirror images of each other:

♦ Both begin with a mention of Passover (Mark 14:1, 12).

♦ Both are sandwiched between reports of human wrongdoing. The anointing at Bethany is preceded by the plot of the chief priests and scribes, and followed by the plotting of Judas (Mark 14:1-2, 10-11). The Last Supper is preceded by Jesus' prophecy of Judas's betrayal, and followed by his prophecy that all the disciples will fall away (Mark 14:18-21, 27-30).

♦ In both, there is an extravagant gift of self that involves a "breaking" and "pouring": as she breaks the jar and pours out the ointment, Jesus *breaks* the bread that is his body and shares the cup that is his blood *poured out.*

♦ In both, Jesus makes an explicit reference to "taking" his body: he tells the disciples, "She has taken my body beforehand to anoint it for burial"; then he tells them, "*Take*; this is my body" (Mark 14:8, 22, emphasis added).

♦ In both Jesus makes a solemn prophetic pronouncement prefaced with "Amen, I say to you." He says in Bethany, "wherever the gospel is preached in the whole world, what she has done will be told in memory of her" (Mark 14:9); then at the Last Supper, "I shall not drink again of the fruit of the vine until that day when I drink it new in the kingdom of God" (14:25).

◆ Both episodes relate to communal memory. In Bethany, Jesus mandates the retelling of the woman's extravagant gift, and at the Last Supper he institutes the Eucharist, the perpetual memorial of his self-gift in the Church until the end of time.[10]

Mark intentionally weaves in these parallels so that the two events shed light on one another. What the woman did for Jesus pointed forward to what he himself would do for us on the cross. *Jesus is God's alabaster jar*, broken for us, pouring out divine life, and now filling the world with his fragrance. Her gift therefore shows whole Church what it means to live Eucharistically: to give a radical, total gift of self, without counting the cost, in response to Jesus' total gift of himself to us.

That gift of self-outpouring love is the gift that Ani and her family gave Pepito, and that he gave them. And they found the Lord's extravagant grace in return. As Ani recalled,

He was so patient and he never complained, but I know he suffered, because everything he felt, I felt it too, and I was prepared for that.

But nothing could have prepared me for the joy that came along with it, the joy that can only come from being so completely united to Christ. Pepito would often have moments when he would spontaneously burst into giggles, or where it would seem like he could not stop smiling. Sometimes his eyes would fix on a point and he would just gaze at one spot and his face would be radiant and his eyes filled with delight. Pepito's optic nerves were so damaged that it's likely the most he could see were big shapes and light and shadows, but we know that he could see things that we can't see. When I looked in his eyes I felt loved beyond comprehension, as if the eyes looking at me were the eyes of Jesus himself. And the very thing that those eyes saw clearly was the face of God.

A few years ago, when Pepito was in the hospital, I lifted him up so the nurses could change his sheets. His hands and feet were pierced with IVs and so many attempts at blood draws over the previous days. He was in terrible pain from a massive pancreatic pseudo-cyst that was forming in his side. Holding him in that moment, I had such a powerful experience of the love of Christ poured out, as I stood at the foot of the cross, united with my son to Christ in his suffering.

Thank God for those like Pepito and his family who give the world a glimpse of the hidden treasure beyond all price. They teach us not to be like the condescending critics of the woman with the alabaster jar, who can only count value in dollars and shekels. They help us understand that true love is love poured out, without counting the cost.

Ani shared at the funeral,

Last week, when the doctors were preparing to intubate Pepito so they could put him on the ventilator, they asked me if he could reach and grasp, if there was any danger of him pulling out the tube. I said no, Pepito could not reach and grasp. He could not try to be anyone other than who God created him to be. He couldn't run away; he could only live each moment perfectly united to the will of the Father. His whole life was an offering of love—a love that he knew because he was so fully united to Jesus. His soul knew no other way. He could not choose anything else.

And those who saw him responded to Jesus in him. I can't count the number of times complete strangers have come up to talk to me because they were so moved by Pepito and wanted to know more about who he was. What they experienced in those moments was the love of Christ. I learned so much from being his mom, from living every day for the last almost eight years in the presence of a saint, holding him, kissing him, caring for him.

But the greatest thing I learned from him is this: Don't be afraid to give God everything. Don't be afraid to pour out every last drop for love of him.

Pray

O Lord, open my eyes, like the eyes of the woman with the alabaster jar, to recognize in you the treasure beyond all price. Help me to give myself to you without counting the cost.

Ponder

1. What does it mean for you that Jesus is God's alabaster jar, broken and poured out for you?

2. Taking an honest look at your life, are you moderate and measured in your response to Jesus, or reckless? Are you willing to go all in for him?

3. Think of someone you know whom the world would consider of little value. How are you called to love and affirm that person?

About the Author

Dr. Mary Healy is professor of Scripture at Sacred Heart Major Seminary in Detroit and a bestselling author and international speaker.

So he came to a city of Samaria called Sychar,
near the field that Jacob gave to his son Joseph.
(John 4:5)

2.

ENCOUNTERED AND ENLIGHTENED

The Woman at the Well

We call it the "fluke in Dubuque." Though best of friends who frequently text, routinely chat, and always long to be scheduled to speak at the same women's conferences, somehow we forgot to mention our upcoming speaking engagements to one another. As I packed my things the night before leaving to speak at the Springtime of Hope: Martha & Mary Women's Conference in Dubuque, Iowa, I checked their website to see who the other speaker would be. In my defense, I usually do this the moment someone asks me to speak at an event. But that spring, my life was overly packed with writing deadlines, speaking engagements, work meetings, driving kids to and from a million sporting events, changing toilet paper rolls (not sure how I'm the only one in our house who has mastered this art), and, well, just life in general.

Reflecting on it today, I chalk it up as a moment of holy procrastination. Had I done my due diligence and inquired who the other speaker would be, the blessing that awaited me would not have been a surprise—and I find that there's something about a surprise encounter with someone I love that lifts my spirits. That evening, as I saw the beautiful face of my sister in Christ, Kitty Cleveland, grace the website, joy sprang up in me and I called her immediately. She was as surprised as I was and just as excited for us to be leading a day of hope together for the women of Dubuque.

Though Kitty's suitcase never arrived in Dubuque, the Holy Spirit did. The conference was anointed in many ways. The Spirit touched hearts—tears were shed, laughter abounded, and, as the women present embraced the teachings, they set out to balance their inner Martha and inner Mary, their active and spiritual lives. We wrapped up the day, and Kitty, grateful that we were the same clothing size and used identical makeup, thanked me for sharing my things and thanked God for the solution. We laughed at how we saw the Lord working on both of us to slow down, embrace our inner Mary, and relish the beauty of the contemplative.

As we entered the home of our dinner hosts, God helped us slow down even more. Actually, he stopped me in my tracks! Bumping into me, Kitty said, "What are you doing?" I was frozen, mesmerized by the stunning painting in the foyer—a breathtaking depiction of the woman at the well. Seeing my head tipped back, eyes staring above the entryway, Kitty looked up and said, "Wow, that is incredible."

And then the craziest thing happened. In my untrained voice, I started singing Peter, Paul & Mary's "Jesus Met the Woman at the Well," a song that was popular four years before I was born. Kitty—who is one of the best singers I know—had never heard the song before. She was in awe, but not because I was mildly in tune or knew the words to the song. Rather, it was the lyrics that amazed her. Based on the story from the Gospel of John, they tell of a woman who had a surprise encounter with Jesus, entered into a relationship with him, and in doing so turned away from her past, began a new life in Christ, and eagerly shared her experience with others.

That spring day in 2014 is long past, but the memory lives on. Whenever Kitty and I are together, inevitably something will make us spontaneously break into "Jesus Met the Woman at the Well." It could be a picture we see, a phrase someone says, a Scripture passage we read, or even a joke someone tells. Ultimately, we know what moves us to sing of this woman: along with our inner Martha and inner Mary, we also have an inner woman at the well. She lives in each of us. She lives in any woman who has ever felt unworthy, longed for a relationship, or thirsted for love. She lives in anyone who has known the transformative power of an encounter with Jesus or longs for such an encounter. No matter where we may be on our spiritual journey, her wisdom is a light illuminating the path of holiness for each of us.

A LITTLE BACK "DROP"

The encounter between Jesus and the woman of Samaria (John 4:4-42) abounds in riches both in its literal sense (its historical meaning) and its spiritual sense (its eternal significance and significance for our lives). So crucial is this meeting between Jesus and the woman that this passage, which is the Gospel reading for Year A, is also an option for Years B and C, especially when catechumens are present. And no wonder—it's a story of encounter, repentance, new life, and evangelization. It's a story of conversion and mission. It is our story.

The Samaritan woman has the longest—and most intimate— conversation with Jesus in all of Scripture. He graces her with one of the richest descriptions of himself and his work. Yet the Gospel writer, John, doesn't mention the woman by name. Instead, he identifies her by where she is from: a "woman of Samaria," as well as by where she is going—to Jacob's well (4:7). As we will see, referring to her by her hometown carries significance.

Knowing someone by name implies a relationship, and Jesus knows her name. He knows everything about her, everything she ever did (John 4:39). Jesus knows her intimately, as becomes clear when the relationship blossoms. He knows that the Samaritan woman feels insignificant and unworthy of love; he knows her struggles, her heart, her gifts, and how she will build up his kingdom.

He knows each of us, too, on the same intimate level. Because this is so, the story overflows with wisdom for us. Let's drink from this fountain, receiving the living waters, as the woman of Samaria did. As St. Ephraim says, "Lord, who can grasp all the wealth of just one of your words? What we understand is much less than we leave behind; like thirsty people who drink from a fountain."[11]

WHERE SHE IS FROM

So he came to a city of Samaria called Sychar, near the field that Jacob gave to his son Joseph. (John 4:5)

When John refers to the woman by her hometown, he's laying the foundation for many lessons that follow. Samaritans and Jews did not get along. In fact, they were longtime rivals. In 722 BC, the Assyrians conquered the ten northern tribes of Israel, brought people from five different conquered nations who married the women, intermingling their pagan ways with the Israelites and forming a new religion that rivaled the religion of the Jews centered in Jerusalem. As they had done since the division of the kingdom in 930 BC, they continued to worship the God of Israel in their own way, with their own temple, priesthood, and canon of Scripture. To the Jews, the Samaritans were heretics and half-breeds, and as such, they did not interact with them.

> By the first century, the worst thing you can call a Jew is a Samaritan. . . . How daring, then, for Jesus . . . to share an extended conversation with a Samaritan woman he meets at a well, then to welcome her whole community as they seek an encounter with him.[12]

By identifying the woman by where she was from, the despised district of Samaria, John demonstrates that this negative, judgmental assessment of an individual is how the world sees. Later in the passage, he demonstrates how the Lord sees. Right off the bat, John sets the stage, calling us to embrace wisdom by looking beyond how we see things in order to see the way God sees.

WHERE SHE WENT

Jacob's well was there, and so Jesus, wearied as he was with his journey, sat down beside the well. It was about the sixth hour. (John 4:6)

John tells us that the Samaritan woman goes to draw water from a well, but, significantly, not just any well—she goes to Jacob's well. For Jewish readers, Jacob's well would instantly bring to mind Old Testament stories that echo a theme of marriage. It is a simple equation: man + woman + well = wedding. Moses meets his future wife, Zipporah, at a well (see Exodus 2:15-22), Abraham's servant meets Rebecca, Isaac's future bride, at a well (see Genesis 24:1-67), and Jacob meets Rachel at a well (see Genesis 29:1-14). In ancient times, if you wanted to meet a good person to marry, the well was the place to be.

In speaking of the woman by where she is going—Jacob's well—the Gospel writer John is making a symbolic reference to a wedding, in which Jesus is the Bridegroom. The

Samaritan woman, while important in and of herself, symbolically represents the Church, the Bride of Christ. And in that role on this momentous occasion, she receives the most incredible wedding gift—insight into the wisdom of God. Amazing! In just two verses, the Evangelist reveals so much by what he says and by what he leaves unsaid.

Baptismal Name?

Though John does not call her by name in the Gospel, Eastern Orthodox Christians have named the Samaritan woman: they call her the Holy Martyr Photini. (Photini means "Enlightened One.") In the Catholic Church, she is St. Photina. Since there is something relational about being called by name, from now on, as we come to know her in a new way, we will refer to her as Photina.

As we have noted, Jesus knows everything about Photina. He knows as he approaches Jacob's well at the hottest time of the day, exhausted and parched from a long journey, that he will encounter a bold, curious, and intelligent Samaritan woman. Imagine hitting complete exhaustion, simply longing for a bit of nourishment and a place to collapse, and knowing if you continue to your destination, you'll meet a feisty Chatty Cathy. How many of us would stop in our tracks or go the other direction in search of peace, quiet, and rest?

Jesus could have thought, "I can't speak with a Samaritan." But he doesn't. He could have thought, "I can't be seen talking to a woman." But he doesn't. He could have thought, "I'm too exhausted to get into a long theological conversation; I just want a little water and rest," but he doesn't. Jesus stays the course and walks to Jacob's well in the heat of the day. There he enters into an intimate relationship with a Samaritan woman; he embraces everything about her: her race, her woundedness, her attributes—boldness, curiosity, intelligence—and her femininity. As Pope St. John Paul II would say, Jesus embraced Photina's gifts of "feminine genius."[13] Jesus taps into her receptivity, sensitivity, generosity, and maternal gifts.

In John's account of the interaction between Jesus and Photina, we see that in the brightest moment of the day, when the sun is directly above, the Son of God brings even more light to those who encounter, engage, and embrace him.

And "so Jesus, wearied as he was with his journey, sat down beside the well" (John 4:6). Photina, for her part, can see Jesus sitting there as she approaches Jacob's well. She, too, could stop in her tracks and avoid the encounter, waiting to draw water when no one is there, but she doesn't. She goes to the well, knowing there is a Jewish man there. Bold move.

Jesus, the ultimate relationship builder, responds to her boldness stating, "Give me a drink" (4:7). Undaunted, her curiosity piqued, she engages in the conversation, asking, "How is it that you, a Jew, ask a drink of me, a woman of Samaria?" (4:9).

Jesus responds to her curiosity, drawing her in deeper. "If you knew . . . ," he begins (4:10). Those three little words would pique anyone's interest. Imagine having coffee with a friend when she leans in to say, "If you knew what they are planning for their big day . . ." Wouldn't your first response be, "What?

Tell me!" That is Photina's reaction at Jacob's well.

Jesus continues, "If you knew the gift of God, and who it is that is saying to you, 'Give me a drink,' you would have asked him, and he would have given you living water" (John 4:10). Her curiosity sharpened, Photina dives deeper into the conversation, stating the physically obvious, "Sir, you have nothing to draw with, and the well is deep" (4:11), while unknowingly asking about the spiritual, "Where do you get that living water?"

LIVING WATER

Photina most likely understands the "living water" to be spring water or running water that will always be present, enabling her to more easily accomplish the activities of daily living such as washing clothes, bathing, preparing food, and quenching thirst.

Jesus said to her, "Every one who drinks of this water will thirst again, but whoever drinks of the water that I shall give him will never thirst; the water that I shall give him will become in him a spring of water welling up to eternal life." (John 4:13-14)

Though Jesus explains the water of eternal life, Photina continues to see from an earthly view. Thinking about the endless water supply that will ease her burden, allowing her to forgo drawing water in the heat of the day, thus avoiding the jeers of the other women gathered at the well in the coolness of the morning, she misses the eternal water Jesus is offering.

It is here, knowing how this story ends, that I want to yell out, "Pho!" (That's what I call her because we're close.) "Pho, you're missing the point! Jesus is taking the conversation to the next level. He is the living water!" Then, I think of how often I miss the eternal because I'm stuck in the here and now, and I cut her some slack. Jesus does more than just cut her some slack; he continues to stir her curiosity and, in doing so, shifts gears, revealing to her that he knows her heart.

> Jesus said to her, "Go, call your husband, and come here." The woman answered him, "I have no husband." Jesus said to her, "You are right in saying, 'I have no husband'; for you have had five husbands, and he whom you now have is not your husband; this you said truly." (John 4:16-18)

Intelligent and tapping into her feminine gift of sensitivity—to see and respond with the heart—she doesn't deny her situation. Photina courageously replies, "Sir, I perceive that you are a prophet" (John 4:19).

Scripture never reveals what her situation was, aside from the mention of five husbands and current lover. But perhaps the Lord is lovingly calling her to recognize her past and reorder her life. If that's the case, it turns out, my friend Pho is a lot like me. When the Lord mentions her husbands, she changes the subject and begins a new discussion. How often have I diverted my attention from my sin so I wouldn't have to change or reorder my life? But regardless of her situation, Jesus continues to pursue her, and, in that pursuit, he takes her to the next level. When Jesus speaks to Photina, he draws metaphors and images exclusively from the five books of Moses and hints, initially, at the person of the Messiah in whom the Samaritans, like the Jews, believe. Jesus meets her where she is spiritually, intellectually, and emotionally, gently helping her go from the earthly view to the eternal. And the moment she herself mentions the Messiah, the Lord immediately jumps in and reveals that he is the One.

"I who speak to you am he." (John 4:26)

Photina embraces this truth completely, so much so that she cannot contain the light within her. Illuminated, she goes in haste, leaving her water jar behind, and runs to the city to share the good news with all. It doesn't matter that previously she hid in the shadows from these people. She is on fire, radiating the love of God, and she wants them to see the man who told her everything she'd ever done. She wants everyone to encounter the Messiah.

And so we see that Jesus, the Bridegroom, meets Photina where she is: physically—at Jacob's well; emotionally—feeling humiliated and like an outcast; and spiritually—seeking the fullness of truth. In doing so, he opens her up to the most intimate of relationships—a relationship with God the Father, God the Son, and God the Holy Spirit. Unlike her relationship with her five husbands or the sixth man with whom she is now living, her relationship with Jesus, the seventh man in this line of men, is a covenant relationship enduring for all eternity. In Scripture, the number seven signifies completion, perfection, and holiness. Photina's relationship with Jesus will ultimately bring her completion, perfection, and holiness.

PHOTINA LIGHTS THE WAY FOR US TODAY

Photina's interaction with Jesus perfectly models how we can grow into a deeper relationship with the Lord and, in turn, grow in holiness. We can follow in Photina's footsteps and encounter the living Lord every day. How often do we let that fact slip by us? Today, if you saw Jesus sitting by a well or . . . sitting at the counter of the coffee shop you visit each morning, what would you do? Would you continue to the counter to place your order? If he asked you to pass the cream and sugar, would you enter into a conversation with him? Would you embrace his teaching? What if he revealed that he knew everything you'd ever done? And what if he spoke of your failures and shortcomings with unconditional love and abundant mercy? After that encounter, would not your heart be on fire, compelling you to run and tell your friends what just happened? I imagine the answer to all these questions is a resounding "Yes!" Well, just as Photina encountered the living God that ordinary day long ago, so can you, every day.

One way we can do that is in prayer as we speak to God, knowing that in Scripture, God speaks to us. Archbishop Allen H. Vigneron captures this reality of God's living word beautifully in his pastoral note on Sacred Scripture:

Reading Scripture is not like reading any other book, because Scripture is a living word through which God speaks to each of us personally, right here and now. "In the sacred books, the Father who is in heaven meets His children with great love and speaks with them." God reveals his heart to us and he longs for us to respond from our hearts. When we read Scripture prayerfully, it becomes a dialogue of love. We listen to God's heart through his word and we respond from our heart in prayer.[14]

A DIALOGUE WITH LOVE

The interaction between Photina and Jesus captures aspects of the dialogue of love that Jesus wants to have with each of us, too. We don't see God face-to-face, as Photina did, but we can encounter him by prayerfully praying the Scriptures in an ancient practice known as *lectio divina* ("divine reading"). This form of prayer allows us to let go of our own agenda and open ourselves to what God wants to say to us, just as Photina did. Centuries ago, a monk named Guigo the Carthusian described *lectio divina* as the steps of a four-rung ladder that lifts us up from earth to heaven.[15] Those four steps are lectio (reading), *meditatio* (meditation), *oratio* (prayer), and *contemplatio* (contemplation). My friend Dr. Tim Gray offers a fifth step, resolutio (prayer in action).[16]

Let's break it down, rung by rung.

Lectio: Encounter Jesus

In *lectio*, we encounter Jesus, the living Word, just as Photina encountered Jesus, the living water. The first paragraph of the *Catechism of the Catholic Church* states that God, "in a plan of sheer goodness," made humanity so that we might all share in his very life. For that reason, God uses every opportunity to draw close to us. Jesus used the hot noon sun, an ancient well, and his thirst to draw close to Photina. He may use a crisp morning, a tranquil lake, or a drink with friends to draw close to us. But he always meets us in his word. And so in this first step, we choose a Scripture passage for prayerful reading. In order to encounter him, to really hear him, *lectio* then encourages us to read the Scripture passage we're considering three times, slowly.

Meditatio: Meditate on the Message

As Photina hung on to every word Jesus spoke, so too should we. In *meditatio*, we engage with the word of God. With focused concentration, we think deeply about the text. Don't let yourself be distracted as you read. Hang on to every word. Pause to look at the word or phrase or scene that grabs your attention. Ask yourself, "What do I hear?" Ponder those particular words or scenes or characters, opening yourself to layers of meaning that you might have missed if you had read quickly.

Oratio: Converse with God

In oratio, we respond to God, as Photina did. She didn't shy away from Jesus; rather, she entered into dialogue with him, responding to his request for a drink: "How is it that you, a Jew, ask a drink of me, a Samaritan?" Just so, as we move from meditation to conversing, we ask questions such as, "What does this passage mean for me in my current circumstance?" or, "Lord, what are you saying to me at this moment?" Photina's simple question—"Sir, where do you get that living water?"—took her further spiritually than she could have ever imagined. The same can be true for us when we dare to enter into a conversation with Jesus.

Simply put, this is our prayer. It can be a prayer in our hearts, a vocal prayer, or a prayer written in a journal. It can be a few words or a more lengthy conversation, like Photina's. Either way, it is a dialogue with God, who has invited us into a relationship of love.

Contemplatio: Rest in the Word and Let It Transform You

In the heat of the day, Photina lingered in conversation with Jesus, a lingering that led to the knowledge that "God is spirit, and those who worship him must worship in spirit and truth" (John 4:24). The Holy Spirit was at work transforming her heart. By the grace of God, *contemplatio* takes place in us during silent prayer that expresses love for God. As the *Catechism* explains, "Contemplative prayer is *silence*, the 'symbol of the world to come' or 'silent love.' Words in this kind of prayer are not speeches; they are like kindling that feeds the fire of love" (2717). . . . a fire fueled by the Holy Spirit.

Resolutio: Act with Renewed Confidence, Conviction, and Hope

On fire with the good news, Photina ran (with haste) and gave her testimony.

So the woman left her water jar, and went away into the city, and said to the people, "Come, see a man who told me all that I ever did." (John 4:28-29)

That is the power of an encounter with Jesus. Once we receive God's love and grace, we are empowered to go forth and share that experience—we are on fire to witness to others. The word of God is our Jacob's well, from which the Living Waters flow eternally. Imagine the spiritual "exercise" we'd get every day if we ran from that well to share Jesus!

A SPLASH OF THE FEMININE GENIUS

Photina demonstrates what it means to be a disciple of Jesus, equipped with the joy and zeal necessary to engage in the new evangelization. In this, she is a model for all women who have encountered Jesus. Photina teaches us to be open and receptive to a relationship with the Lord, to be sensitive to him and engage him with our heart and mind, to embrace the love of the Lord and generously share it. Overcome by God's love, Photina ran to share the news of Jesus with those she initially avoided. That is precisely what we should do. We, too, in love with the Lord, can't help but want to share him with everyone we meet. As Pope St. Paul VI wrote in his apostolic exhortation *Evangelii Nuntiandi*:

> The person who has been evangelized goes on to evangelize others. Here lies the test of truth, the touchstone of evangelization: it is unthinkable that a person should accept the Word and give himself to the kingdom without becoming a person who bears witness to it and proclaims it in his turn.[17]

We can all relate to Photina in various ways. But let's especially relate to her in this way: nothing stopped her from sharing the good news of God's love, and nothing should stop us. She is a woman with a past who, perhaps, has done things she's not proud of. She is a woman who at times feels alone. She is a woman who doesn't think she is good enough or has much to give and who often feels unprepared, ill-equipped, and insignificant. She is a woman who feels like she is out of her league and doesn't belong. She is a woman who believes she is unworthy of love. She is a woman who isn't doing anything grand. Instead, she is doing what comes naturally to her as a woman, something that sustains life. She is drawing water.

In that act, that simple daily act, she has an encounter. And with one encounter, a woman coming to draw water is turned into a woman ablaze with the love of God. She is a woman in the "new" evangelization of Samaria.

Jesus shared so much of himself with Photina. Some may ask, "Why would he tell so much to someone so insignificant?" The answer is simple. Because to him, she wasn't insignificant at all. Jesus wanted to shower his love on her—to tell her everything. That's how he felt about Photina, and that's how he feels about you.

On this journey of life, we are all seeking, even if, like Photina, we may not know it. We may be seeking peace, forgiveness, acceptance, company, or encouragement. Perhaps we are seeking answers to questions we hold in the depth of our heart. Or we may be seeking a break from all the activity around us. Though we may search for those things, ultimately, we all seek a transformative encounter with the living water.

St. Augustine, in his *Confessions*, wrote, "Our hearts are restless until they rest in you, O Lord." Jesus knew well Photina's restlessness; he knew her soul was thirsting for him, the living water—the Divine Life, which ironically quenches one's thirst while at the same time igniting a burning passion. That is why he "had to pass through Samaria," an area Jewish people avoided: to encounter a woman scorned by her neighbors while he rested at Jacob's well, a place where covenant relationships begin (John 4:4). Jesus wasn't just wearied from his long journey and looking for a sip of water; he was thirsting for the woman at the well so that she might thirst for him, just as he thirsts for us. "God thirsts that we may thirst for him" (*Catechism*, 2560).

> The theme of thirst runs throughout John's Gospel: from the meeting with the Samaritan woman . . . to the Cross, when Jesus, before he dies, said to fulfil the Scriptures: "I thirst" . . . Christ's thirst is an entranceway to the mystery of God, who became thirsty to satisfy our thirst. . . . The Samaritan woman, . . . represents the existential dissatisfaction of one who does not find what he seeks. . . . ; her going to and from the well to draw water expresses a repetitive and resigned life. However, everything changes for her that day, thanks to the conversation with the Lord Jesus, who upsets her to

the point that she leaves her pitcher of water and runs to tell the villagers: "Come, see a man who told me all that I ever did. Can this be the Christ?" (Jn 4:29).[18]

Something about a surprise encounter with someone you love lifts your spirits and makes you eager to share the experience. Pope Benedict XVI said, "There is nothing more beautiful than to be surprised by the Gospel, by the encounter with Christ. There is nothing more beautiful than to know Him and to speak to others of our friendship with Him."[19] Those two sentences capture the story of the Samaritan woman and, at the same time, remind us that there is nothing better than having an encounter with Jesus, embracing his friendship, and running to tell others about him.

St. Photina highlights a beautiful lesson for women: may we never underestimate the role of women in evangelization because God doesn't. He chose to reveal himself as the Messiah to a woman—a receptive woman who didn't turn away from him but engaged in a conversation and embraced his teaching, who was sensitive and saw Jesus with her heart, and who was generous in sharing the good news with all.

A woman came to a well, not knowing the spiritual healing she needed, and she left proclaiming the Messiah, joyfully lighting the way to holiness for many. What could be more maternal than caring for many souls? May we all be that woman.

PRAY

St. Photina, your thirst for the Living Water changed you forever. Pray with us, dear St. Photina, that we will recognize encounters with Jesus and allow him to pour his mercy upon us, quenching our thirst and transforming our hearts. As our hearts open wide, we pray the Lord will ignite a fire within us to spend time with him in his word and learn from him always. And following in your footsteps, may we joyfully run and share our love for Jesus with everyone we meet. May our love for the Lord radiate a light in us—a light so lovely that people can't help but want to know the source of it! In Jesus' name, we pray. Amen.

PONDER

1. The story of the woman at the well is a call to look beyond how we see things in order to see the way God sees. Can you recall a moment in which your perspective on a situation or a relationship was changed? Who or what contributed to this experience?

2. Following her conversation with Jesus, Photina wanted everyone to encounter the Messiah, and she went in haste to share the good news with the very people she once avoided. Can you recall any encounters with the Lord that

led you to act or speak in ways that you normally would not have? Or can you recall times where the love of God pushed fear away from your heart?

3. Jesus chose to reveal his true identity to an ordinary woman who didn't think she was good enough or had much to give, and who felt like she didn't belong. How does this story empower you and encourage you to embrace Jesus and share the good news with others?

ABOUT THE AUTHOR

Kelly Wahlquist is the founder of the national women's ministry WINE: Women In the New Evangelization and the director for the Archbishop Flynn Catechetical Institute at The Saint Paul Seminary in the Archdiocese of Saint Paul and Minneapolis.

"Wherever you go I will go,
    wherever you lodge I will lodge.
Your people shall be my people,
    and your God, my God." (Ruth 1:16)

3.

ENTRUSTED TO TRUST

M y husband and I met when we were still in high school. He was handsome and intriguingly different. While I was a Texan and had never moved from the home my parents bought when I was six months old, Dale, on the other hand, was born in Venezuela to an American couple, a geologist and his wife. He was raised in Angola, Nigeria, South Africa, and London, and had moved to Texas as another stop on his colorful life journey. We became friends right away, and I introduced him to everyone I knew.

Eventually we fell in love and married while still in college. I should have known that someone with that kind of a past would never be happy to settle down in dear "little" Texas, when there was a whole big world just waiting to be explored. Right after graduation, we packed up our few things and headed to Washington, DC, to start our adventure. He told me we would live on the East Coast for one year, move to the West Coast for one year, and then move back to Texas or possibly on to Africa to be missionaries.

That all sounded so exciting. But I can remember the fear that struck my heart as we headed east and crossed the border into Louisiana. "Here we go!" I thought. And yet, as a Southern Baptist who studied and loved the Bible, I drew courage as I remembered the many women in Scripture who similarly set out on adventures, conquering their fear and attuned to the will of God. One of my all-time biblical favorites was Ruth the Moabite. Her story, as it turned out, was destined to play a part in my own story.

We drove and drove until we arrived in Washington, DC. We stayed in Dale's uncle's row house while looking for jobs. The city was so strangely "other." Everyone lived close together and yet no one said "Howdy" as they passed by, or even "Hello." Growing up in one neighborhood and going to the same school and church for nearly my entire life, I knew just about everyone I had ever come across. Here, I didn't know a single soul.

My husband immediately found work as an architect and started making new friends at his office. I sat home, alone, with no job, no friends, and very little money. To make matters worse, within only a few weeks of moving to DC, a freak blizzard hit town on my birthday in November and paralyzed the city for days. It was freezing and I thought, "If this is what it's like *now*, I'll never make it through January!"

I was a stranger in a very strange land. I was incredibly homesick, and life was not going *at all* like I expected. We joined the closest church that was affiliated with our denomination, but there were no other young couples and very few native English speakers because the pastor spoke Portuguese. (The service was translated into several languages.) Our best (and only) friends that we made as a couple were three older Brazilian ladies, two of whom worked in nearby homes and one who worked for the embassy. I begged to move back to the familiar. I wanted to go HOME! NOW!

My husband said we would . . . eventually.

Desperate and very lonely, I cried out to God for help. Then God, in his sweet and tender way, drew my attention to something on my hand that gleamed when it caught the sunlight. I hadn't even noticed or thought about it for a very long time because I wore it on my finger every day. I looked down and beside my golden wedding band (which *should* have been enough for me to come to this conclusion), I saw the ring that I had bought when we lived in Texas—when my life was sunnier and full of hope. I read the inscription engraved on it in Hebrew:

"Wherever you go, I will go."

Ruth 1:16 to the rescue.

The passage acted as a reality check for me. By God's grace, I realized I needed to change my attitude and start counting my blessings, even if life was very different from what I had thought it would be. From that moment, I decided that instead of feeling sorry for myself and only looking inward, I would make more of an effort to see why God had placed us here to begin with and try working with *his* plan instead of dreaming up my own. In prayer, I asked for the grace to hit restart and begin again—no more pity parties!—and to draw my strength and my "happy" from God.

Hope and Loyalty

In Scripture, we see that the verse—powerful in its own right—continues, soaring even higher:

> "Wherever you go I will go,
>   wherever you lodge I will lodge.
> Your people shall be my people
>   and your God, my God.
> Where you die I will die,
>   and there be buried." (Ruth 1:16-17)

Though these words are often read at wedding ceremonies, surprisingly they weren't originally spoken in a romantic setting. The woman pledging her devotion is Ruth the Moabite, and the person to whom she is speaking is Naomi, her mother-in-law. Ruth's loyalty to Naomi, grounded in hope, unfolds against a tragic background that ultimately reveals the faithfulness of a God who never abandons his people.

The story begins around 1150 BC in one of the gloomiest eras of Israel's early history—the time of the judges. Wickedness ruled as the people fell into a cycle of disobedience and idolatry, followed by God's judgment, the people's repentance, and a few years of peace before the cycle began again. During this period, famine strikes the region of Judah, driving Elimelech (whose name means "my God is king"), his wife Naomi (whose name means "sweetness" or "pleasantness"), and their two sons to the country of Moab, about fifty miles east of their home in Bethlehem.

Elimelech dies, unfortunately, and the two sons marry Moabite women named Orpah and Ruth. After ten years, the sons also die, leaving their wives childless and their mother in a foreign land among foreign people. The women, each now a widow and without children, have no one to carry on the family line or to care for them, in a culture and time when women were economically dependent on men. Naomi, too old to bear children, explains that she will return to her people because she has heard that God has ended the famine that had brought her family to Moab. She tells her daughters-in-law to return to their mothers in order to find husbands among their own people and their own gods. Orpah, though hesitant, returns to her family. But Ruth clings to Naomi declaring, in that most eloquent statement, "Wherever you go I will go" (1:16). With a flicker of hope in her heart, Ruth accompanies Naomi on their journey into the unknown to begin again.

I have often wondered why Ruth didn't return to her own people and do the easier thing, like Orpah. Was it because she had found what she had always been looking for in the people and ways of the God of Israel? Unlike the culture in which she grew up, the children of Israel didn't engage in child sacrifice or cultic sexual practices. The wisdom, strength, and sweetness of Naomi, whose words were always saturated with talk of the God of Israel, were perhaps so compelling to Ruth that she was willing to forgo her own people, take a leap of faith, and pledge herself to her mother-in-law. In doing so, maybe she hoped to find more of these God-focused people in Naomi's land. But still, Bethlehem was a very long, hot journey for two destitute and unaccompanied women to make by foot. And for Ruth, the customs and practices of Israel were sure to be drastically different from those of her homeland in Moab.

KINDNESS AND GRACE

The story continues as the two women arrive in Bethlehem at the beginning of the barley harvest. Naomi is the talk of the town, though grief and the harshness of life have taken their toll. Scripture states,

The whole town was excited about them, and the women asked: "Can this be Naomi?" (Ruth 1:19)

Naomi is distraught and perhaps taken aback by the sight of her old friends and how well they have fared, and in the realization that they hardly recognize her. She has been deeply affected by her trials.

She said to them, "Do not call me Naomi ['Sweet']. Call me
Mara ['Bitter'], for the Almighty has made my life very bitter.
I went away full, but the LORD has brought me back *empty*."
(Ruth 1:20-21, emphasis added)

Blaming God is never pretty; neither is a lack of gratitude
in failing to see what God has graciously provided.

Naomi doesn't seem to recognize—or at least she fails to
acknowledge—the precious gift God has given her. Instead of
being thankful for the gift God has entrusted to her in Ruth, and
for all that Ruth had relinquished in order to care for her, griev-
ing Naomi calls her hands "empty." Ouch. Naomi, passionate,
emotional, and overwhelmed by life, seems unable to recognize
the significance and worth of her daughter-in-law. The famine
has moved from an external event to an internal one. Her *soul*
is desolate. Devoted, loyal Ruth, who did not abandon Naomi
in her greatest time of need in Moab, still does not abandon her
now in Bethlehem.

Ruth refuses to be offended and overtaken by negative
emotions. She could easily have become sullen and withdrawn.
Instead, she takes action, acting in the opposite way, lovingly
blessing Naomi by taking the initiative to fill Naomi's "empty"
hands. She practices *hesed*, a Hebrew word that means, essen-
tially, *kindness*. A fuller definition captures the deeper meaning:

> *Hesed* is often used in Hebrew in connection with other words
> which bring out its meaning, such as *hesed-emet* (steadfast,
> dependable love), *hesed-sedekah* (righteous, holy love) and
> *hesed-yesua* (rescuing, saving love).[20]

The word *hesed* appears frequently in the Old Testament, echoing again and again in the story of Israel. It speaks of God's covenant loyalty to his beloved people, the love and kindness that he gives even when it is underserved or unexpected. Ruth embodies this characteristic, mirroring the beauty, tenderness, and goodness of God, in a way that bears the fruit of blessing as opposed to bitterness.

Ruth sets out to glean in order to find food for Naomi and herself and "happens," apparently at random, to choose the field of a relative of her late father-in law that is ripe for harvest. And so, not knowing what to expect, Ruth sets out and begins her work.

TRUST AND HUMBLE OBEDIENCE

The last act of the story of Ruth is almost too exquisite to comprehend. Mercy, love, redemption, favor, and transformation all come into play and foreshadow what was to come in the fullness of time in salvation history with the birth of our Savior.

The owner of the field where Ruth gleans is named Boaz. Looking out into his fields, Boaz notices a stranger. He asks the man overseeing the harvest about her, who tells him that she is a Moabite woman, Naomi's daughter-in-law, and that she has worked all morning with very little rest. Not only does Boaz hear of Ruth—he gets "a complete account" of all she has done for Naomi (2:11). He approaches her and says,

"May the LORD reward what you have done! May you receive a full reward from the LORD, the God of Israel, under whose wings you have come for refuge!" (2:12)

Boaz takes pity and tells his workers to make special allowances in the fields for her, keeping a protective eye on her and purposefully dropping grain as they harvest so that Ruth has plenty to gather. Boaz himself gives her some roasted grain to eat at mealtime, and she wraps some of it up to bring home to Naomi.

When Ruth tells Naomi that she has gleaned in the field of a man named Boaz, we, the readers, can see the faithfulness of God beginning to unfold. So, it seems, can Naomi. She exclaims, "This man is a near relative of ours, one of our redeemers" (2:20)—simply put, a relative who steps up to help a family member in need.

As the days pass, Naomi encourages Ruth to return again and again to Boaz's fields. Ruth trustingly and humbly obeys. Ruth's energetic expressions of trust and devotion toward Naomi plant seeds of hope inside Naomi's heart that begin to take root and grow. Scripture makes clear: the trust Ruth and Naomi put in one another flourishes as they work together to ensure their future. In Ruth, Naomi has found a loving and trusted young friend—one ready to take risks and to act boldly and decisively for the good of them both (and eventually for us all). In Naomi, Ruth has found a wise and compassionate mature voice to guide her that will ultimately lead to something so much greater than either one of them could imagine.

At the end of the harvest season, Naomi instructs Ruth to do something *extremely* bold, not to mention dangerous, because neither of them is assured of the outcome. Naomi tells Ruth to go, late at night, under cover of darkness, to the threshing room floor where Boaz would be sleeping in order to guard his grain at harvest's end. Once he's asleep, she should uncover Boaz's feet and quietly lie down next to them, awaiting his response. If she were to find favor in his eyes, all would end well, but if she did not, her reputation and her safety could be in peril.

Ruth faithfully follows Naomi's advice. Boaz, startled, awakens in the night and is surprised to find a woman at his feet. Ruth, not knowing what will happen next, identifies herself and says he is a redeeming kinsman. Boaz, to her relief, responds with praise:

"May the LORD bless you, my daughter! You have been even more loyal now than before in not going after the young men, whether poor or rich. Now rest assured, my daughter, I will do for you whatever you say; all my townspeople know you to be a worthy woman." (3:10-11)

Boaz covers Ruth with the "wing of his cloak," showing her his favor; and in the morning, fills Ruth's cloak with grain so that she can, in turn, fill Naomi's empty hands (see 3:9, 15). According to Jewish custom, Boaz is eligible, as Ruth's kinsman redeemer, to buy the field that belonged to Ruth's father-in-law and that Naomi had put up for sale. In doing so, he would also marry Ruth. Boaz assumes this responsibility, and he and Ruth are married. The Lord blesses Ruth, who did not have children during her marriage to Naomi's son, and she now conceives. She and Boaz are able to carry on the family name and to once again fill Naomi's empty hands, but this time with the most precious fruit, a son named Obed (which means "worshipper"). Exuberantly, the town's people declare that Ruth, the Moabite, is worth far more than seven sons to Naomi!

The book concludes with a brief genealogy, an essential part of Ruth's story and a tribute to her faithfulness. Ruth and Boaz's son Obed becomes the father of Jesse, and Jesse becomes the father of King David, the exalted forefather of the prophesied greatest King of all times, Jesus Christ.

GOD'S *HESED* TODAY

The story of Ruth has continued to echo in my life from the moment I glimpsed my ring and made the words of Ruth my own: "Wherever you go, I will go." In my case, I had a renewed commitment to going with my husband wherever God led us. As it turns out, we never moved to the West Coast, to Africa, or back to Texas. We settled in, got to work, joined an amazing church with lots of young couples our own age, and had oodles of Christian friends, many of whom, by God's grace, we helped to lead to Christ. We had three beautiful girls, and I had a thriving women's ministry. Our hands and lives were full! What could be better than that?

But there was more. "What, Lord? You want me to do *what*? You want me to follow you *where*?" After the birth of our fourth child, I began to feel a tug at my heart to do something that

I knew was going to cause issues, to put it mildly. I had been teaching a women's Bible study that the Lord had inspired me to begin many years before. One day, a dear friend came up to me during the study and boldly said, "I have finally met someone who loves Jesus more than you do!" I was shocked! She went on to say, "He's a Catholic priest." Then I was really shocked.

I didn't personally know any practicing, on-fire Catholics. I knew a few Catholics, but they never talked about their faith. In an attempt to prove my friend wrong, I met with the priest and was stunned to discover that she was right. He did seem to love Jesus more than I did. When I asked him what the secret was, he told me, "It's the Eucharist."

Then he challenged me to go to an Adoration chapel, where the Blessed Sacrament is reserved for prayer. I began to ask God to show me the truth about the Catholic faith that I knew so little about and what to do next. I had extreme anxiety because this was all so unfamiliar to me and was making me question the theology on which I had built my life and ministry. From that day, I avoided going anywhere near an Adoration chapel! But since one had just been built onto the back of the Catholic church where we sent our children to school, I now made a point of running past it each day.

Finally, the Spirit forcefully compelled me to go in. Acting against everything I had been taught in my Protestant upbringing, I trustingly and humbly obeyed and did what I felt the Lord was calling me to do. Like Ruth, not knowing the outcome, I did what I thought was *right* but was not at all easy. I knew that if my Protestant Bible study leadership friends got wind that I was becoming "Catholic curious," it could create turmoil in my ministry, not to mention in my family and my life.

Quite fearful, I prayed before I went into the Adoration chapel that day: "Lord, if what I am about to do will offend you in any way, I pray that you forgive me in advance. But if you are really in there, I pray that you will let me know right away, because I believe that this will be the only time that I go in." I took a deep breath, unlocked the door using the code that a friend had shared with me, and stepped inside.

"No lightning bolts so far," I thought.

I went in and knelt down and opened the little doors on the tabernacle as my friend had instructed me to do. "So far so good," I said to myself.

It felt really peaceful, not scary like I thought it would.

After a long time, I began to pray, "Here I am Lord. I have come trustingly out of humble obedience, doing what I think you have asked of me. If you are really in here, I ask that you please make yourself known to me because, as I said, I don't think I will be coming back here any time soon."

And then it happened. Whooooosh!

Like a river of love shooting out of the tabernacle—that's the only way I know to describe it—I had the most overwhelming experience of love that I have ever known. I felt picked up and buoyed by love. It was around me, in me, under me, through me. I was floating in love, only I don't think I ever left the ground. I was so super saturated by love that I have no idea how long it lasted, but I knew I never wanted it to end.

I began to laugh and then to weep. I told the Lord how very sorry I was for all of my faults, failures, and judgments of his beloved Catholic people. I wept out of happiness that he loved me enough to become present to me in this spectacular way. I cried because I never wanted to leave that little room. I had no idea what was next, but I knew that all of my fears and all of the unknown were nothing in comparison to being known and loved by him. He was my Kinsman Redeemer. He saw me, he knew me, he loved me, he bought me with the price of his own dear life, and he gave me the courage I needed to take the next steps. He covered me with the "wing of his cloak"— with his wing of love—and I was in love.

By his grace, the Lord drew me into the Catholic Church. I needed to overcome many, many fears of the unknown and address many questions, but in trust and humility, I obeyed. We (he and I) overcame my fears together, and I found the answers to my questions. Even in the darkness of the unknown, my fears gave way to trust, in obedience.

Blessings and Joy

Tradition states that the fertile, flourishing field of Boaz, the field in which Ruth gleaned, is adjacent to the field in Bethlehem where the angels announced the birth of Christ to the shepherds. Bethlehem was the ancestral home of David, and before him, Jesse, and before him, the home of Ruth, Boaz, Naomi, and baby Obed. The story of redemption—the salvation of the whole world—flows through a mixed ethnic linage of Jesus

Christ through figures such as Ruth, a Gentile and Boaz, who was half Canaanite, due to his mother, Rahab, being a prostitute from Jericho. Only God could weave such an intricate, beautiful, story from such diverse and often tattered threads.

Just as in the story of Ruth the Moabite, the sweet fruit of trust and humble obedience continues to bring us life today. The story of salvation offered to us through Jesus is indebted to the sacrifices of a long line of faithful, often unknown, people committed to God's will regardless of the cost. That story unfolds today in your life and mine. May we be like them—these ancestors in the faith—displaying hope and loyalty, kindness and grace, trust and humble obedience. By God's grace, may we flourish, ever-green, used by him to love all those we encounter.

And each time we go forward to take the Eucharist and say *Amen*, each time we receive Jesus, Body and Blood, soul and divinity, may Christ be born anew in our hearts and in our physical bodies. Jesus came in the flesh through the *yes* of Ruth and then, later, through the *yes* of Mary, his mother. He continues to come today through your *yes* and mine.

PRAY

Dear Lord, the words of Ruth, "Wherever you go I will go," are much easier said than done, especially when the path you lead me on is dark and full of unknowns or bright and full of things I do not want to do! Lord, please help me to trust you so unwaveringly that, by your grace, I can step out confidently in faith—like Ruth, full of hope for the good things to come. Lord, I trust in you; help me to trust in you more. Lord, I have hope in you; help me to hope in you more. Lord, I love you; help me to love you more. Lord, please give me an overflowing, abundant increase of your Spirit, because anything less than you is not worth the ask. Thank you for hearing and answering this prayer. Amen.

PONDER

1. Have you ever found yourself feeling like a stranger in a foreign land? Or where life was not going at all like you expected? How was God present to you in that season, and how did the season pass?

2. Ruth's trust and devotion toward Naomi plant seeds of hope inside Naomi's heart, and Ruth looks to Naomi for wisdom of what to do. What aspect of their relationship speaks to you?

3. Jesus is our Kinsman Redeemer, as Boaz was to Ruth. When, like Ruth, we place ourselves in need of his covering, Jesus covers us with his love, his salvation, and his redemption. What does this image evoke for you?

About the Author

Melissa Overmyer is the founder of Something Greater Ministries, which provides opportunities for people to encounter God through prayer; Scripture study; community; and the teachings, traditions, and spirituality of the Catholic Church.

Rahab the harlot, and her father's household,
and all who belonged to her, Joshua saved alive.
(Joshua 6:25)

4.

THE FALL OF THE WALLS

Rahab

One of my most profound understandings of Scripture came with the realization that before the fall, Adam and Eve had an eye-to-eye gaze.[21] They were at peace within themselves and in harmony with each other, with nature, and with God. Adam and Eve had an eye-to-eye gaze, conscious of one another's dignity, aware of their unique roles in the order of creation. Their mutual confidence and trust in each other enabled them to serve as a team.

Although their harmony was soon shattered at the fall, it was a glimpse of complementarity, which is seen between men and women throughout Scripture, sometimes in wholly unexpected ways.

Meet Rahab, the Prostitute

The Exodus has taken place. Moses led the Israelites to the edge of the Promised Land, but because of his earlier disobedience to God at the waters of Meribah, God told him he would never enter the land.[22] Moses remained beloved by God, and from Mount Nebo God let Moses glimpse the Promised Land from afar. Moses died, leaving Joshua to lead the Israelites into the Promised Land. He prepared them to take the land, sending two spies into Jericho, the first city the Israelites would take. This is where we join the story.

The spies went to the house of Rahab, a prostitute. Scripture doesn't shy away from this description, using the word "prostitute" or "harlot" in reference to Rahab three times in the Book of Joshua and several times elsewhere in the Bible. Some scholars believe that she may have been a woman who practiced prostitution associated with fertility goddesses and religious rites. Such so-called sacred prostitutes worked within a respected tradition. Other commentators suggest that she might have been an innkeeper, a role that sometimes involved prostitution as a side feature. Perhaps she was a young widow with a family to support and doing what she could to stay afloat in a profession she and others despised. Or perhaps she had been forced into prostitution as a young girl or had left prostitution behind but the townspeople wouldn't let her forget.

However, for me, I identify with her as a prostitute—meaning the contemporary understanding of *prostitute*. It is not an insult to her; it is just the beginning of her story. I won't tell you the end of the story right now, but stay tuned—it's fantastic!

Her identity aside, she and the people of Jericho were about to encounter the Israelites face-to-face. Rahab, along with the rest of the residents of Jericho, has heard all that the God of the Israelites had done for them—the story of their escape from Egypt, the parting of the Red Sea, their time in the desert, their battles, everything. How had those in Jericho heard what God had done for the Israelites? Trade routes, gossip—word gets around, especially when the Israelites' God has been so strong and faithful. As for Rahab, it seems natural for the spies to seek her. As a prostitute, she would be particularly aware of the comings and goings of Jericho, and she was used to receiving men.

The spies are hidden by Rahab, as they are being sought by the king of Jericho. Once the spies are safe, she tells them,

"And as soon as we heard it, our hearts melted, and there was no courage left in any man, because of you; for the LORD your God is he who is God in heaven above and on earth beneath." (Joshua 2:11)

In essence, everyone in Jericho knows the power of God and their hearts have melted in fear. Rahab's heart has also melted, but she has been left with amazing wisdom and courage.

She goes on to claim her salvation. And she goes even further; she claims the salvation of her family.

"Now then, swear to me by the LORD that as I have dealt kindly with you, you also will deal kindly with my father's house, and

give me a sure sign, and save alive my father and mother, my brothers and sisters, and all who belong to them, and deliver our lives from death." And the men said to her, "Our life for yours! If you do not tell this business of ours, then we will deal kindly and faithfully with you when the Lord gives us the land." (Joshua 2:12-14)

I often ponder this passage. Rahab believes in God but we, the readers, don't know if her family believes. It seems they have heard of God, but have their hearts melted in fear or in courage, as Rahab's heart melted? If they do not believe in God, then Rahab's faith is all the more astounding. The faith of one woman, Rahab, saves many—her family.

The act of saving the family was dramatic as well. The spies gave her conditions and a sign.

"Behold, when we come into the land, you shall bind this scarlet cord in the window through which you let us down; and you shall gather into your house your father and mother, your brothers, and all your father's household. If any one goes out of the doors of your house into the street, his blood shall be upon his head, and we shall be guiltless; but if a hand is laid upon any one who is with you in the house, his blood shall be on our head." (Joshua 2:18-19)

The spies guaranteed Rahab's and her family's safety if they remained in her home. If anyone left, they would not be saved. Additionally, she would need to hang a scarlet cord from her window. Remember, Rahab lived in the walls of Jericho.

Remember, the *walls* would fall—the very walls where she lived.

For six days, the Israelites marched around Jericho once each day. On the seventh day, they marched around seven times. As they blew trumpets and shouted, the city walls began to fall. The trumpets, the shouts, the wall falling—what a shocking chain of events. When the people of Jericho first realized the stones and bricks were falling, did anyone try to put them back in place? When they discovered the collapse was too rapid, what did they do next?

Go back to Rahab and her family. They must have heard the walls falling as well. Were they panicked in the apartment? Did they want to run? Did Rahab have to convince her family to remain? Did they *all stay*? Did any run? Imagine the deep faith of Rahab. When she heard the walls falling, she recalled the pact she had made with the spies. She remained where she was, knowing it was the condition of her salvation.

Rahab was a woman who had been used by men, but the spies saw her dignity and recognized her intelligence. They greeted her with an eye-to-eye gaze, a level gaze, which continued during that intense moment as she made the arrangement with them. She might have recalled that gaze as she heard the walls fall. Rahab knew the God of the Israelites was the true God, and she deeply trusted his messengers. What a woman of strength, wisdom, and courage!

The Israelites Save Rahab and Her Family

And Joshua said to the two men who had spied out the land,
"Go into the harlot's house, and bring out from it the woman,
and all who belong to her, as you swore to her." So the young
men who had been spies went in, and brought out Rahab,
and her father and mother and brothers and all who belonged
to her; and they brought all her kindred, and set them outside
the camp of Israel. (Joshua 6:22-23)

It must have been an overwhelming moment for the family.
Most likely, they hadn't met the Israelites until they came to
save them. They had to trust Rahab. Had they ever looked
down on her, or taken advantage of her financially? What was
it that made them trust her? Was it just that she offered them
the only possible way to survive the siege? Or was it something
different? I like to think that her gaze played a role. I suspect
that when Rahab told her family of the pact she had made with
the Israelites, there was something in her eyes—a deep abiding
trust, courage, and certainty. Rahab was an evangelist to her
family, and they believed.

I teach Scripture to high school students; one of the great
joys of teaching happens when students ask me about something
I've never considered. We were discussing the destruction of
Jericho in class one day, and I pointed out that the destruction began while Rahab and her family were still in her house,
and it continued as they were saved. A freshman, Molly, asked,

"How did Rahab and her family continue to believe that the Israelites' God is good after he had the Israelites destroy everyone in Jericho?"

What a great question. After a moment, I said that Rahab was all-in. She looked forward, not behind. Another student said that Rahab was the *opposite* of Lot's wife, who was told not to turn around, yet did and became a pillar of salt. Rahab, on the other hand, went forward to her future.

Later, that evening, I was having dinner with Melissa Overmyer and, without giving her my opinion, I asked her my student's question about Rahab's ability to believe in spite of the destruction of those around her. Melissa reminded me that wherever chaos is present, the Holy Spirit hovers above it and brings new life. Yes! The destruction of Jericho was a new beginning—the area of Jericho later became a part of the Promised Land. As painful as the destruction of the city was, Rahab didn't allow the chaos to paralyze her; the promise of new life gave her the strength to trust and follow.

Rahab Embraces the Future

But Rahab the harlot, and her father's household, and all who belonged to her, Joshua saved alive; and she dwelt in Israel to this day, because she hid the messengers whom Joshua sent to spy out Jericho. (Joshua 6:25)

Rahab marries Salmon, an Israelite, and becomes the mother of Boaz, a good man who will marry Ruth. The genealogy in the first chapter of Gospel of Matthew lists Rahab in the bloodline of Christ—a Gentile, a prostitute who recognized the hand of God at work among the Israelites, met the spies with an eye-to-eye gaze, and plotted their escape while intervening on behalf of her family. She then followed the Israelites, married one of them, and became an ancestor to the Messiah. What a testament to God's mercy. Although she was a prostitute, that did not define her. Her repentance, her belief, and who she *became*—this is who she *is!* She is a daughter of the Father—and one of the great-grandmas to the Son!

Centuries later, Rahab receives praise in the Letter to the Hebrews. Rahab took a risk by receiving the spies. She hoped; she had faith. Hebrews says:

By faith Rahab the harlot did not perish with those who were disobedient, because she had given friendly welcome to the spies. (Hebrews 11:31)

Perhaps this peace came with the eye-to-eye gaze of dignity she exchanged with the spies.

MY JERICHO WALLS

There were many dark years in my life—seventeen that were utterly black. I was Catholic, but in name only, far from the

Church and her teachings. I desired happiness, which included the hope for a good man to enter my life. However, I know now that what I desired and what I thought I deserved were in stark contrast to each other. I allowed a parade of bad men to use me. In the midst of the bad men were five good men. Oddly, I wondered why the good men would be good to me. Their calmness and goodness didn't leave me off-balance, so I convinced myself they were boring, even though we had wonderful times. Also, I became nearly suspicious of them; why would they treat me so well when so many other men didn't? In my utter confusion between what I desired and what I thought I deserved, I chased the good men away as quickly as possible. The parade of bad men joined me in my life of promiscuity, sorrow, and loneliness, although I emphatically claimed that I was having *fun*.

In a sense, I lived in my own Jericho where the walls of fun were seemingly impenetrable. In a way, just as Rahab lived in the walls of Jericho, I lived in the walls of my promiscuity, not really in the city of "fun" proper. I thought so little of myself and men thought so little of me that they never invited me to join them in their city of fun. Although I tried to convince myself that life in the walls was exactly where I desired to be, the walls were really a place of hiding. I was never really a member of their society. Sadly, I was only there to be of service to them. I was always seeking love, but was left with wound after wound.

In May of 1988, I decided to quit sleeping with men. Oddly, I didn't think this was the part that made me so sad. I remember that I felt some relief, but I had left many other bad habits untouched, which allowed other pain to continue. Certainly, during this time, my dignity was not a consideration, nor was my relationship with God.

In January of 1989, I was raped and became pregnant. My life was one of utter desperation. I was still inside the seemingly protective walls of my Jericho of *fun*, but now I found that I couldn't escape. I was trapped, and none of it was fun; it never had been, but I couldn't admit this truth. Instead, I built an additional wall to protect all of it. I was in a new fortress of denial and refused to let anyone into my sorrow.

Fear and denial pushed me and, relying on the world's advice for pregnancy due to rape, I had an abortion. What no one tells you: although you leave the abortion clinic no longer pregnant, it's as if you have agreed to carry an anvil of sorrow above your head for the rest of your life. If your elbow becomes weak, you only need to repeat the abortion mantras to strengthen it. "It's my body; I can do what I like." "It's just a clump of cells," and so on.

In my fear and denial, my life of promiscuity began anew. A year later, I was pregnant again. Having never dealt with the first abortion, the second abortion seemed like the only answer. I left the clinic again, no longer carrying a child, but carrying a second anvil of sorrow. The anvils of sorrow were so heavy, yet *fun* was my mask.

It was August 19, 1998, and I was prepared to kill myself. I had the means to do it; the note was written. I called my mother to hear her voice one last time, trying to make small talk. She had mom hearing. She knew something was wrong and said she was on her way. But on her way still meant five hours and she didn't yet have a cell phone. What an awful drive for her, suspecting but not knowing what I intended to do.

Five hours left me with plenty of time. However, I knew that my mom would be the one who would find me, and I knew that she didn't deserve to have the memory of her dead daughter emblazoned in her mind.

I said to God, "I'll give you one shot at this."

He didn't need more; he had been waiting.

The worst day and the best day came together. It was the worst day because the anvils of sorrow fell on my chest, and I couldn't breathe. It was the best day because I finally had to admit the truth, "I killed my babies," which finally allowed the healing to begin.

The Holy Spirit had been hovering over the chaos of my life. Just as in Jericho, it *looked and felt* worse as the walls of my fortress of hiding and denial fell. The walls that I thought protected me were my jail. Entering a life without destruction was unknown to me; it was frightening, but my Jericho had been leveled.

Through it all, my mother's love for me, and all of her work and prayers, were directed toward my redemption. She greeted me with an eye-to-eye gaze, recognizing my innate dignity, even though I couldn't return her gaze in the same way.

Needing a place to rest, I returned to Church. However, I didn't intend to stay, and there were times when I left, returned to the rubble, and attempted to rebuild Jericho. I wanted to return to what was known, but even as I put a few bricks together, I understood I was reassembling my destruction. I would turn to

God and follow him and his Church again until, eventually, I could no longer leave. The Church was home.

In the spring of 1999, I went to Bishop Paul Dudley for my first adult confession. He had been a friend of my father since they were in eleventh grade at the high school seminary until my father left the major seminary several years later. The two of them lost touch until Bishop Dudley became the bishop of the Sioux Falls Diocese where he had confirmed me, and I had come to know him. It had been at least seventeen years since my last confession, but I confessed everything to the bishop. I was afraid he would kick me out, but he deeply understood what I was only beginning to understand—forgiveness. At the end of the confession, he said, "Alyssa, imagine the rejoicing in heaven today for one sinner coming home!"

As I was leaving, he stopped me and said, "Alyssa, God has forgiven you. Now, go home and do the hard work of forgiving yourself."

What? I was never going to forgive myself! My guardian angel must have put a hand over my mouth—I didn't tell the good bishop what I was thinking.

RAHAB SPEAKS TO MY HEART

Somewhere along the line, I lost the sense of my dignity. The parade of bad men never had the eye-to-eye gaze of dignity with me, which sadly didn't even register with me. My mother continued to seek my eye-to-eye gaze, but I couldn't return it. Ultimately, in the Sacrament of Confession with Bishop

Dudley, the eye-to-eye gaze was restored. The surprise was that he was not trying to restore it with himself, but with God. In the Sacrament of Confession, Bishop Dudley was the conduit that allowed my gaze to return to God's gaze.

From time to time, the sorrow has returned. For example, once, more than twenty years after the abortions, I received information about a physical wound that was nearly certainly a result of one of the abortions. I was surprised by the intensity of the sorrow, which seemed to hit my chest like the waves of an ocean. Although I knew that I had been forgiven, my tears flowed anew. I missed my children who I never knew. For solace, I wrote to my dear friend, Fr. Paul Murray, OP, telling him that my heart was an open wound again. He had the most beautiful advice, telling me to allow the wound to become a womb of blessing, a place of new life.[23] Letting the wounds become a womb—this has become a call to my heart.

Rahab's life was in chaos before the walls of Jericho fell, but she had given her *fiat*, her *yes*, to the unknown God of the Israelites. Whatever lies or sufferings or sorrow filled her past, she refused to let them destroy her future; she inspires me. On that terrible day when I was about to take my life, I gave the weakest *fiat* only to protect my mother, but my whole life changed. Looking back, I can see the Holy Spirit working throughout the dark years. He hovered over my chaos, waiting for me to turn to him. Finally, finally, I did.

When Rahab left the walls of Jericho, she began a life that included motherhood, placing her in the bloodline of Christ. Although I refused physical motherhood, I have now experienced spiritual motherhood through my many students, one of whom is now a priest; he has called me a spiritual mother. God is the God of Mercy!

Through his hands, and the hands of every priest, the Eucharist is consecrated. In the *smallest* way, as I receive Communion, I stand by my sister Rahab. She was physically in the bloodline of Christ. I am spiritually there as I receive the Body, Blood, Soul, and Divinity of Christ.

Rahab came into the story of salvation history in an odd way, and so have I. She was a woman of courage, trust, and wisdom; may I also be.

PRAY

My dearest sister Rahab, you have helped save me from the disorder of my Jericho walls. So many of our sisters in Christ have similar wounds as mine. Please gather them in your heart, hang the scarlet cord that led to your salvation, and call on the saving grace of the God of the Israelites to save them as well. You know the Holy Spirit hovers above their personal chaos, waiting for their *fiat*. Be a guide to the wounded, that they may know the dignity of an eye-to-eye gaze with the Father, and they may allow their wounds to become a womb of new life.

Ponder

1. Imagine Rahab's deep faith and courage as the walls were falling—the very walls within which she lived—as she waited for the Israelite spies to make good on their promise to save her and her family. Have you ever experienced a time when you were waiting for a promise of God to come to pass and had to exercise great faith and courage?

2. As painful as the destruction of Jericho must have been to her, Rahab didn't allow the chaos to paralyze her. Instead, she chose to trust in the promise of new life. How can we prepare our hearts to find strength in the promises of God, so that when pain or suffering comes, we too can keep our gaze on Christ?

3. Following her first confession in many years, Alyssa heard the words, "Imagine the rejoicing in heaven today for one sinner coming home!" Imagine your heavenly Father saying these words to you. How does it feel? What is your response?

About the Author

Alyssa Bormes is an educator, author, speaker, writer, and emcee.

Esther put on her royal garments and stood in the inner courtyard, looking toward the royal palace, while the king was seated on his royal throne in the audience chamber, facing the palace doorway. When he saw Queen Esther standing in the courtyard, she won his favor. (Esther 5:1-2)

5.

DRESSING FOR SUCCESS

Esther

God uses all sorts of ways to draw us closer and into a deeper relationship with him. He knows us better than we know ourselves. In my case, he knows that for most of my life, all the way back to my early childhood years, I was a "girlie girl." My attraction to beauty and bling began with Barbie and friends. My dolls had more clothes and accessories than my mother, my two sisters, and me combined. I also had a great aunt who worked as a seamstress in the garment industry in New York. Aunt Angie helped seal the deal when it came to my fascination with all things fashion. That fascination would eventually play an important role in my life as I pursued my profession as a broadcast journalist and lived in the public eye.

So it isn't any surprise that when I first heard about Queen Esther, she had my attention, as did the Lord. I first became aware of Esther through a beautiful song by the Christian artist Wayne Watson. The title of the tune, "For Such a Time as This," was first released in 1998 and was based on what are probably the most well-known verses in the Old Testament Book of Esther. The verses center on a pivotal point in Esther's life when she is challenged by her cousin Mordecai to risk her life of privilege and comfort in the king's court in order to save the Jewish people.

[Mordecai] had this reply brought to her: "Do not imagine that you are safe in the king's palace, you alone of all the Jews. Even if you now remain silent, relief and deliverance will come to the Jews from another source; but you and your father's house will perish. Who knows—perhaps it was for a time like this that you became queen?" (Esther 4:13-14)

A MARRIAGE RESTORED AND A NEW PURPOSE

The hit song also came at a crucial period in my own life. In the mid to late 1990s, my husband and I were on an amazing journey of healing and discovery. After a near divorce, God came into our lives and turned our world upside down in an incredible way. Not only did he heal our marriage, but he also (although we didn't quite realize it at the time) was leading us back into the Catholic Church—and not only into the Church, but into ministry! Eventually my husband, Dominick, would become a deacon and I would become a Catholic talk show host, author, and speaker.

Our journey began at a Detroit Pistons basketball game. We attended that game with my boss at the time and her husband, Gene, who just happened to be in a men's Bible study. I was only interested in the fact that I was sitting in the front row at a championship game that was being broadcast live on TV. But God had other plans. The Holy Spirit was working through Gene as he invited Dom to that Bible study. As my husband explains when we share our testimony, no one was more surprised than him when he blurted out, "Sure, that sounds like a great idea. I would love to come!" The moment he said those words, he wanted to turn around and ask, "Who said that?" My husband is an engineer and by nature and not someone who makes decisions quickly, especially with something as unique as an invitation to study Scripture with dozens of men he didn't know. But because he had said yes, he attended the class.

That Bible study was the first and most important step that led to our eventual reversion to the Catholic faith. Studying Scripture reintroduced my husband to God and the Church. It gave him the necessary foundation to weather the upcoming storms in our marriage and the crises that would bring us both to our knees. That class changed Dominick for the better, and it made *me* want what he had. It was the catalyst for the long journey home to each other and Jesus.

During this time of awakening, we began attending Bible studies and numerous parish activities. Our interests were also changing and becoming much more Christ-centered, and that included our media choices. The Christian radio station was the new norm in our household. I found Wayne Watson's Christian hit to be so moving that it really piqued my interest in Esther. Of course, who wouldn't be challenged and encouraged by Mordecai's words to her? I certainly was. Those particular verses tugged at my heart, especially since my husband and I were at such an interesting period in our own lives.

But there was something else that attracted me to this biblical royal rock star: she knew that although clothes don't make the person, they certainly have their place—and at times, that place can be a prominent one.

As part of our journey back to God and each other, my husband and I had many moments of self-reflection, and what we saw in the mirror wasn't pretty, to say the least. We certainly did not reflect, at that time, the light of Christ through our marriage. We had both been raised Catholic, but we quickly left the Church in the dust as our careers began to flourish. Many of my own struggles were caused by my focusing only on the outside. While we were both practically obsessed with worldly success, my efforts on making it big as an on-air personality caused me to become shallow. My life lacked balance, and we both paid the price for that selfishness.

Yet Esther's example helped me regain that balance by realizing that beauty needs to be expressed both inside and out, with the emphasis first on the inside. "Dressing for success," as we will see from additional examples of Queen Esther, is not only for those ministering or working in the Church, the media, politics, or other types of public arenas. The way we present ourselves makes a difference. It means something. Queen Esther knew this and so did another Queen, the Queen of All Saints, our Blessed Mother. As Christians, we are always called to take the high road: to present ourselves to God and each other in the best light, not for our own gratification or glory, but for the glory of God.

DRESSING FOR SUCCESS

Whether we like it or not, there is a need for appropriate attire for particular occasions. A recent story makes this point. During the early fall of 2023, a debate occurred in the United States Senate over appropriate dress. It was sparked by a senator from Pennsylvania, John Fetterman, whose wardrobe of choice is a hoodie and gym shorts. Bipartisan backlash boiled over after dress requirements were quietly relaxed by Senate Majority Leader, Chuck Schumer of New York.

More than four dozen senators sent a letter to Schumer, raising concerns about the relaxed dress code. "The world watches us on that floor and we must protect the sanctity of that place at all costs," the letter reads. "Allowing casual clothing on the Senate floor disrespects the institution we serve and the American families we represent." In covering the dress code debacle, *The New York Times* pointed out how much we stand to lose when dress codes are loosened:

> How we dress telegraphs intricate messages to those around us, as well as to ourselves—messages we receive and interpret constantly, consciously or not. There is no such thing as "total freedom" of dress, only different registers of meaning, which

are entirely context dependent. Just as words make sense only relationally—in sentences and paragraphs—garments have meaning only in relation to other garments. A tuxedo'd guest at a wedding is unexceptional, nearly invisible. A tuxedo'd guest at a picnic is a spectacle.[24]

Too often, as the piece wrote, we might be too quick to dismiss what clothes represent in a civilized society that's becoming more uncivil almost daily:

It's true that in recent years, offices have loosened their dress codes, embracing all kinds of workplace attire. But the Senate is more than just a "workplace." It represents the highest level of our country's government, whose actions are watched by and hold consequences for the entire world.[25]

The senators eventually passed a resolution formalizing business attire as the proper dress code. The new written rules require a coat, a tie, and slacks for men.

"Whoa, Nellie," you might be thinking. "What is all this talk about our outward appearance when in so many places in the Bible, we're told it's only what inside that counts?" You could point to what God said to Samuel about his chosen one, David:

"Do not judge from his appearance or from his lofty stature, because I have rejected him. God does not see as a mortal, who sees the appearance. The LORD looks into the heart."
(1 Samuel 16:7)

And even the Lord himself reminds us in John's Gospel to go deeper:

"Stop judging by appearances, but judge justly." (John 7:24)

OUR OBSESSION WITH OUR APPEARANCE

I get it. But we do indeed live in a world obsessed with appearance. We are not only obsessed with looking at others, but also obsessed with looking at ourselves. It's estimated that there are some 93 million selfies taken daily. And the average person takes at least 450 selfies per year. One study found that we're so hooked on trying to get more attention on social media that we even put ourselves and others in harm's way, just to get what we think is that must-have shot.

According to one study, some 41 percent of those surveyed have already risked their safety doing just that.[26] And then there is the obsession in the opposite direction, with research showing that a majority of women think poorly of themselves. So poorly of themselves and their appearance that a *Glamour* magazine survey conducted several years ago found that 97 percent of those questioned admitted to having at least one negative thought about themselves daily, telling themselves they're fat or ugly or needed to be a size 2 or even smaller. The pressures from the media, especially the rise of social media, even prompted the Dove soap company to launch a major campaign, "Real Beauty," nearly twenty years ago that's still going strong. It began with advertising and then moved into a self-esteem project providing a variety of tools for parents and educators to help young women and girls grow in confidence and challenge negative body images and stereotypes that oversaturate our culture.

The idea of "dressing for success" involves clothing ourselves in ways that help us feel competent and look professional as well as presentable. Did you know that there are a number of studies, even one that dates all the way back to the 1950s, that show that just dressing more professionally, say in business attire rather than more casual wear, makes a big difference in the way you're perceived, and not just on the job? The way we dress, at least according to this research, can impact the way people respond to us.

In this study conducted in 1955, the researchers had their subject dress in two types of outfits. The first time around, he was dressed in casual clothing, including pants and a shirt. He wasn't dressed in rags or dirty clothes, mind you; he was just more casual than the second time around when he stepped out onto the street in a designer business suit. He was instructed to cross the street against the traffic to see how many people would follow him, and if the attire made a difference. Well, it made a big difference! According to the study, more than 3.5 times the people followed in his footsteps when he was dressed in those designer duds compared to the more casual apparel.

I find it helpful, and perhaps it's because I am still in the public eye, to think of myself as always "working," so to speak, for the Lord. I'm always on the job. "Dressing for success" is a way of life for me. And as we will see from other examples in Scripture and the powerful example of Queen Esther, it can be a major component, or layer (pun intended) for our daily conversion of heart.

For all of you who are baptized into Christ have clothed yourselves with Christ. (Galatians 3:27)

As Christians, Jesus is to be our everything. We are to love him with all our heart, soul, mind, and strength as we're told in St. Mark's Gospel (12:30). Jesus, and our embrace of Church teaching, must be the driving force of our lives. It must direct all our actions and decisions, large and small. This is what it means to be "clothed in Christ." This concept of "dressing for success," I believe, has a double meaning. We "dress for success" by preparing ourselves properly on the inside and then reflecting that love of God on the outside. It's both, not one or the other.

ESTHER, THE ULTIMATE STYLIST

I consider Queen Esther the ultimate stylist. There are so many reasons to look to this beautiful young woman for guidance. As I share some of her story, notice how she has her priorities in order. She is stunning to look at but extremely humble. She is a queen who was chosen for the harem of the Persian king because of her good looks. She won great favor and admiration from him because of that beauty. But her ultimate King was the Lord God. Her story is the story of the deliverance of the

Jewish people that came about because she knew how to dress in a way that would produce a successful outcome.

Her cousin Mordecai comes to inform Esther of a plot to kill the Jews, a plot hatched by Haman, an evil servant of the king. In chapter 4, before Mordecai reaches out to Esther, we see him tearing his garments, dressing in sackcloth and ashes, and walking through the city crying loudly out of concern and love for their people. He then goes to the royal palace, and through messengers, implores Esther to go before the king. Esther, in turn, reminds her cousin that anyone who goes before the king without first being summoned would be sentenced to death. However, this doesn't stop Mordecai from encouraging her to speak up: "Who knows—perhaps it was for a time like this that you became queen?" (4:14).

What happens next is yet another example for us to follow. Although it is not written in the actual verses, it is not difficult to read between the lines and see how Esther is already think-ing and praying deeply after her exchange with Mordecai. She's "dressing for success" by praying, fasting, and totally submitting to God's will, come what may.

Esther sent back to Mordecai the response:

"Go and assemble all the Jews who are in Susa; fast on my behalf, all of you, not eating or drinking night or day for three days. I and my maids will also fast in the same way. Thus prepared, I will go to the king, contrary to the law. If I perish, I perish!" Mordecai went away and did exactly as Esther had commanded. (Esther 4:16-17)

A SPIRITUAL WARDROBE

Esther's honesty with the Lord is another stylist's guideline to add to our "spiritual wardrobe." It's not easy to realize that your next step could be your last. Esther shows us that we should never be afraid of being real with God:

Queen Esther, seized with mortal anguish, fled to the Lord for refuge. Taking off her splendid garments, she put on garments of distress and mourning. In place of her precious ointments she covered her head with dung and ashes. She afflicted her body severely and in place of her festive adornments, her tangled hair covered her. Then she prayed to the Lord, the God of Israel, saying: "My Lord, you alone are our King. Help me, who am alone and have no help but you, for I am taking my life in my hand."
(Esther C:14-15)

Meekness, a contrite heart, and a healthy fear of the Lord are the other stylist "tips" to remember, compliments of Queen Esther. She was clothed in the Lord from head to toe. She had covered herself in prayer and fasting. Despite her prominent position, she obviously told herself often, *God is God, and I am not.* And although she accepted her place in public, she did not relish in it nor walk around the palace lording it over her maidens.

Courage was another part of Queen Esther's wardrobe. Mordecai had implored her over the years not to reveal her Jewish faith to the king, as he feared for her life and the lives of their people. She could have told her cousin, "Thanks but no thanks." Up until the point when she learned of the plot to wipe out the Jews, she had the best of both worlds. She had all the comforts that came with royalty and the ability to worship God in her own private way. Esther could have easily told her cousin to find someone else to go before the king; she could have ignored the specific call on her life in order to save her own skin. Esther is so relatable because her decision was not easily made; she didn't march on down to see the king right away. Who wouldn't be having anxiety attacks if they were in her shoes? Even after praying and fasting for days, her mortal anguish remained.

And if you read further in the Book of Esther, you will see that she was so distressed, she fainted as she was going before the king. She may have been shaking in her boots or maybe, in her case, her fancy slippers. But she did have the guts to go forward and honor the opportunity to make a difference, despite the possible and not-so-pretty outcome.

So after preparing herself as best she could on the inside, Esther then began to dress for the occasion on the outside, including what I imagine properly included quite the impressive bling:

On the third day, ending her prayers, she took off her prayer garments and arrayed herself in her splendid attire.
(Esther D:1)[27]

Esther's appearance pleased the king, so much so that he allowed her to come forward and make her plea, and even offered her half of his kingdom in the process. And this is what I love about Esther. She knew that dressing for the occasion wasn't the only step, but it was an important one in achieving success. I encourage you to read the entire Book of Esther to get to know her and to learn more about her arduous but successful journey in saving her people.

MARY, THE GOLD STANDARD

Mary has visited us all over the world, and she has used her image to connect with the people to whom she appears. There have been numerous approved apparitions, but one of the most prominent, Our Lady of Guadalupe, occurred in 1531 to St. Juan Diego on Tepeyac Hill, just outside present-day Mexico City. The Virgin Mary appeared as an Aztec girl, and her clothes were decorated with many symbols familiar to the Aztec culture. The darker color of her skin and the very detailed way she was dressed, including a flower with four petals that represented the supreme goddess of the Aztecs, were crucial as they helped in passing on her message. She appeared as one of them, not as a foreigner, and this helped lead to the conversion of the indigenous peoples—even bringing an end their practice of human sacrifice.

The tilma, which Juan Diego used to collect the spectacular roses that miraculously sprouted on Tepeyac Hill in the middle of winter, is venerated by millions annually at the Guadalupe shrine. This piece of clothing, which should have deteriorated over the centuries, is not only still intact but displays a brilliantly colorful image of Our Lady on the fabric. The intricate detail that went into the way our Blessed Mother presented herself so perfectly on Tepeyac Hill is mind-blowing and a reminder that God works through beauty, including the beauty of how we choose to clothe our bodies. Our Lady of Guadalupe's presence in Mexico several centuries ago caused the Aztecs and others to reflect on their own lives and prompted incredible change.

A modern-day example pertaining to the importance of the image of our Blessed Mother would be the iconic image of Our Lady on top of the University of Notre Dame's golden dome. A dear friend of mine and student at the university, Elizabeth Hale, whom I consider to be more like my niece, wonderfully articulated this point in an article she penned for the student newspaper, *The Irish Rover*. The piece, entitled "Our Gold Standard," highlighted the reasoning behind the detailed and expensive work done in 2023 to re-gild the dome. As Elizabeth explained, some "1,250 delicate strips of imported Italian gold sheets" had to be manually applied to the top of the dome."

She continued,

> Essential to the mission of the university is the pursuit of excellence and pursuing exterior beauty is a crucial part of this excellence. The re-gilding of Our Lady is one manifestation of this pursuit. . . . A symbol of Our Lady's protection of the university, it is important that the statue accurately reflect the woman that it symbolizes. It was not sufficient for Our Lady to be *good enough*. She had to be beautiful. She had to be excellent.[28]

WE ALL HAVE A PLATFORM

When I was working as a reporter and anchorwoman in the 1980s and 90s, we regularly had stylists who came in to consult with the on-air talent. Meeting with the stylists was not optional; it was written in our contracts. We had to sign on the dotted line and agree to follow their guidelines in terms of colors, style, and the length of our skirts and dresses. We had a very particular dress code.

And that dress code was not only for our time on the air waves. Our contracts also included a morality clause. Given the state of the secular media today and the way talk show hosts and news anchors dress and act, a morality clause seems like an anachronism. However, in my day (and granted, that was decades ago), "dressing for success" had to be our standard on and off the air. We were public figures representing a television station, and we were reminded regularly that we had a responsibility to the station and the public to always put our best foot or shoe forward, so to speak. People were watching us—and not just during the Five or Six O'Clock News.

Let me share a real-life story that brings this point home. In 2004 my parents were in a serious car accident that put them in the hospital for several weeks. The wreck occurred not far from where we live in metro Detroit. My mother called me from her cell phone sounding very shaken up and asked me and Dominick to come help them.

Since my mother was able to dial the phone and carry on a conversation, my husband and I were not prepared for what we saw when we arrived. My mother had somehow lost control when she was driving and smashed into the side of a local restaurant. (As a side note, we nicknamed that restaurant, Rosie's Drive-Thru Diner, after my mom, and shortly after the accident, the owners placed three very large brick planters outside the building in the very spot where Rosie made her mark, just in case someone like her decided to come cruising by again. But I digress.) There was glass and debris were everywhere. Several police cars were on the scene as well as an ambulance. My father was on a stretcher and barely able to speak. And there was my mom standing in the middle of this mess that looked like a scene out of an Arnold Schwarzenegger action movie. She was arguing loudly with the EMS crew. She had blood all over her raincoat, and it didn't take a medical degree to realize she was in bad shape. But like the typical tough Italian that she was, she insisted that she and my father were just fine and did not need to go the hospital.

That's when the police and emergency personnel approached us and begged us to try and talk some sense into her. The conversation with my mom quickly elevated as she continued to refuse to get in the ambulance "Ma, please," I shouted. "You must get help and you must get it now. Please get in the ambulance!" I was so concerned for her that I hadn't noticed a large crowd had been gathering nearby. It was a busy area very close to the corner of where two major avenues intersect and where several pubs and restaurants are located.

Suddenly, I heard someone in the crowd say, "Why is Teresa Tomeo yelling at that poor old lady? That's just terrible." When I turned to see who had made the comment, I saw several strangers staring at me and shaking their heads, as if I were the bad guy, even though all I was doing was trying to get my parents help. That didn't matter. It was Teresa Tomeo, the media personality, doing what appeared to be something they thought was very unbecoming and right there for all the world to see. Oh, and did I mention I had been off the secular media airwaves for about five years at that point?

As Christian women, we are representatives, even "broadcasters of the faith," more so. now than ever before. Thanks to the explosion of the internet and countless outlets, most of us have platforms We're all public figures on some level and people are indeed watching us, and not just at Mass or Bible study. What type of photos and comments do we post or share? What is the tone of our emails and texts? Are we dressing nicely and modestly? How do we act toward each other in public?

These are questions we need to be asking ourselves regularly, since by virtue of our Baptism we are all called to evangelize. As Christians, we have signed a spiritual contract with the Lord, including a special dress code as well as a morality contract. And thanks be to God, we have incredible "stylists," such as the beautiful, humble, and courageous Queen Esther who can help us honor that contract.

Note that even Jesus had something to say about the need to dress for success:

"When the king came in to meet the guests he saw a man there not dressed in a wedding garment. He said to him, 'My friend, how is it that you came in here without a wedding garment?' But he was reduced to silence." (Matthew 22:11-12)

Most of us wouldn't think of showing up at a family or friend's wedding in shorts or flip-flops, unless the invitation specifically called for guests to dress in a very casual beach-vibe theme. That would not be dressing for the occasion. "Dressing for the occasion" means understanding what's appropriate to wear for a given event. There is a strong analogy to the idea of dressing appropriately in this verse. Jesus, of course, was talking about not being properly dressed in the spiritual sense, but the idea carries over into how we present ourselves in public as well. If an invitation calls for black tie for men and formal wear for women, you would be insulting the hosts by ignoring the dress code and attending in blue jeans.

A Question of Balance

At the end of the day—for Esther and for us—it's not about extremes. We shouldn't let that pendulum swing too far one way or the other. Don't get obsessed with looks and appearance where it almost destroys your life, as it did in my case. But walking around in hoodies and gym shorts 24/7 is not the answer either. Esther's looks, magnificent wardrobe, and coveted lifestyle were not the focus of her life. She did not, however, toss them aside. She had balance as she saw that they were gifts to be used wisely. She also understood that before we tackle anything on any given day, it all begins with prayer. She had her priorities in order.

That's what I love so much about worshipping Christ within the one, holy, and apostolic Church. The Church is all about balance. One of the questions I often receive, especially when I am being interviewed by the secular press on a matter pertaining to the faith, is a question that really gets my Italian up. "Are you a liberal or conservative Catholic?" My response is always the same. "I'm Catholic. And I try every day, many times unsuccessfully, to embrace and practice all the teachings of the Church because all the teachings work together in harmony in uplifting the dignity of each human being."

The Church doesn't tell us to throw the baby out with bathwater; it strives for balance and moderation. For example, while our current and recent popes have given incredible direction and guidance on the proper usage of the media, they also understand its role in evangelization, education, and cultural development. The Church also doesn't tell women to forget about dressing nicely, but to dress modestly and to think about how our appearance might be affecting those around us.

The Psalms remind us that we are queens for more than a day:

Daughters of kings are among your ladies of honors; at your right hand stands the queen in gold of Ophir. (Psalm 45:9, NRSVCE)

When we become Christians, we are grafted in the royal family, the family ruled by the King of Kings and the Lord of Lords. We are queens and princesses, minus the bejeweled tiaras and the purple robes. We're crowned with the blood of the Lamb of God and given countless treasures passed on to us in Scripture, Church teaching, the sacraments, the saints, and two thousand years of the Church founded by the King himself.

It doesn't mean that we must go broke buying Chanel or Gucci. It doesn't mean we should obsess about our reflection in the mirror. It does mean remembering who we are, as daughters of the King, and dressing the part. We are his royal representatives. So let's strive to be more like Queen Esther and do our best to wear it well, from the inside out.

Pray

Lord, thank you for calling me your beloved daughter. Help me to see myself the way you see me and to carry myself with dignity and honor. Grant me the courage to approach you with confidence, and to display you to the world in the way that I dress and communicate with others.

PONDER

1. What does the idea of "dressing for success" mean to you?

2. How much emphasis do you place on how you present yourself?

3. What can you learn about "dressing for success" from the inside out from Queen Esther?

ABOUT THE AUTHOR

Teresa Tomeo is an author, a syndicated Catholic talk show host, and a motivational speaker with over thirty years of experience in TV, radio, and newspaper.

"Let it be with me according to your word."
(Luke 1:38)

6.

Graced for Heavenly Collaboration

Mary at the Annunciation

A young woman seeks me out for spiritual direction. She is a devout Catholic, having spent several years as a missionary in Africa. Back in the United States she is turning her heart toward family life, having long felt called to be a wife and mother. In the past six months, she has been dating a fine Christian man. He is not Catholic, though he seems open to Catholicism. He is supportive of her devotion to the Rosary and Eucharistic adoration. Occasionally he attends Mass with her and she joins him for Bible studies at his church. They seem unusually well suited to one another in many practical ways, in temperament and tastes, in their desire to serve the poor and to live very simply. She notes that there's an abundance of grace and chemistry, "like we were made for each other," she says. Naturally, they start thinking about marriage.

But there are areas where the boyfriend resists her faith, areas that would create division in their home if they married. These are primarily about raising the children as Catholics, including baptizing them as infants. As she speaks, I hear the tension in her voice, can see it in her face. She is wrestling. Questions wash over her, straining her heart and soul.

"Do I marry him or not?" she wonders. "He's such a good guy, and it's so hard to find good men these days. Am I crazy to pass him up? Why would God bring us together and let so much between us be so good if I'm not supposed to be with him? Am I hearing the Lord on this or not?" Her questions are sincere and worthy.

Another woman, married more than thirty years, tells me point blank, "My marriage is killing me." Her husband has been unfaithful with multiple women since the very beginning of their relationship, something she only learned after ten years of marriage and three children. He is emotionally abusive and financially a tyrant. She has undertaken every kind of therapy and healing prayer and retreat that there is to address their troubles; her husband, however, will not participate honestly in these interventions and his behavior is only getting worse. It's unclear whether this is due to addiction or another mental illness, malice, or some combination of these things. "He's killing me," she says again, and I believe her. She is frail and drawn. She looks exactly like someone who has been abused and betrayed in the most intimate ways for more than thirty years.

"I want so badly to know the Lord's will," she says, the tears streaming unchecked. "Do I stay and just take it? For the kids, for our grandkids? Will it benefit them if I stay? I just need God so badly to tell me his will."

THE CHARACTER OF CHRISTIAN ASSENT

Who among us has not been faced with the need to make a similarly critical decision? We have all sought the Lord's will with an earnest heart over matters of great importance—decisions about vocation, relationships, finances, health, our children, our work, our world. We want to be obedient, to do the right thing, to be good and faithful servants, but the way isn't clear so we beg heaven, "Please, just tell me what to do."

More than any other woman in the Bible, it is Mary who has taught me the most about setting a course for my life *with* the Lord, collaborating and co-creating *with* heaven. I turn most often to her, in union with the Holy Trinity, asking not just to make good decisions but to make *graced* decisions. And to be patient— sometimes heroically patient—as the mystery of life unfolds and I wait for the clarity necessary to make those decisions.

And in a particular way, I look to Mary at the Annunciation, when an angel approached with an impossible idea, and Mary, still so young, responded with an astonishing answer that resulted in the greatest collaboration between heaven and earth that the world would ever know: the Word made flesh. Through

Mary's assent, the Incarnation became a reality in her being and her body. In the world. And her Son would change everything.

Adrienne von Speyer,[29] the great Swiss convert, makes an important distinction about the character of Mary's decision in that moment when she agrees, "Let it be with me according to your word" (Luke 1:38). Von Speyer writes:

> [Mary] lets herself be completely penetrated by this assent precisely because it is the first Christian assent. Her assent of self-surrender is the opposite of the self-destruction of despair; it contains within itself the complete fullness of faith, love, and hope. . . . What God demands he never demands without a reason; *he will use it*. But he does not use it in such a way that the giver is thereby consumed, lost, disintegrated. He takes nothing away in such a way that he leaves the giver prostrate, as if consumed. He fills the one who has emptied himself *with divine life, with divine mission*. . . . Obedience, chastity, and poverty are in no way a suicide of the human spirit but rather its life in a new grace.[30]

We do not want to pass quickly over the character of Mary's assent. First, we note that Mary's assent at the Annunciation is the prototype for every moment of assent that follows thereafter for every Christian heart, including yours and mine. We want to study it, pray with it, imitate it, and join our hearts to it. Second, the invitation to Mary at the Annunciation is the invitation to all of us. Caryll Houselander would call it "Christing the world."[31]

The point is, how will we allow the Lord to take root in us and to grow within us, forming us and the resources and gifts of our lives so that he might be birthed again and again in a world that needs him so much? In short, how will we bring the love and truth of Jesus to others? Every decision we make throughout our lives contains this same question within it.

And finally, the assent the Lord invites us to never destroys; it upbuilds. It does not decimate us—it showers our lives in ever-expanding graces and helps us to embrace the most satisfying, most meaningful life we could dream of. This will not be a life devoid of pain, but it will be a life filled with joy and awash in eternal meaning. In collaboration with God, we are not annihilated for his will. No, we are made more, we are magnified, we become more ourselves. Mary at the Annunciation teaches us this with confidence and joy.

We would do well to enter often into the great, unspeakable mystery that is the Annunciation in order to better understand this essential truth: God desires to *co-create* with us. He does not want slaves; he wants collaborators. This life of creative collaboration unfolds through our ever-deepening assent to God.

A RIVER OF ASSENT

Through the Annunciation, Mary is named as "highly favored," and she learns more about who she is, the mother of God. We want to look for similar clarifications in our own annunciation moments.

Let's rest here in the word of God, mindful that it is living and active. Let us pray, *Come, Holy Spirit*, as we read from the Gospel of Luke:

In the sixth month the angel Gabriel was sent by God to a town in Galilee called Nazareth, to a virgin engaged to a man whose name was Joseph, of the house of David. The virgin's name was Mary. And he came to her and said, "Greetings, favored one! The LORD is with you." But she was much perplexed by his words and pondered what sort of greeting this might be. The angel said to her, "Do not be afraid, Mary, for you have found favor with God. And now, you will conceive in your womb and bear a son, and you will name him Jesus. He will be great, and will be called the Son of the Most High, and the LORD God will give to him the throne of his ancestor David. He will reign over the house of Jacob forever, and of his kingdom there will be no end." Mary said to the angel, "How can this be, since I am a virgin?" The angel said to her, "The Holy Spirit will come upon you, and the power of the Most High will overshadow you; therefore the child to be born will be holy; he will be called Son of God. And now, your relative Elizabeth in her old age has also conceived a son; and this is the sixth month for her who was said to be barren. For nothing will be impossible with God." Then Mary said, "Here am I, the servant of the LORD; let it be with me according to your word." Then the angel departed from her. (Luke 1:26-38)

I recently took a graduate-level course about Mary, and we spent hours looking at some of the most celebrated renditions of the Annunciation in art. These masterpieces teach us a great deal about the Church's traditional understanding of this moment. Many, for example, show Mary reading Scripture or a book when Gabriel appears;[32] that is, the angel broke in upon her while she was in prayer, studying, readying herself for the

Lord's mission. Mary was deeply engrossed in his word, preparing herself for this infilling of divine life—the implication being that she could engage the angel because she had been preparing her mind and her soul for encounter with the Lord, even though she didn't know the particulars of what that would be.

Surely this detail alone teaches us something. Do we know the voice of heaven? Are we steeping ourselves in God's word so that we recognize the Lord's voice when he breaks into our daily lives to speak to our hearts? Do we take seriously our preparation and readiness for the divine life and mission Jesus calls us to? Do we lean on the ancient wisdom of the Church to help us respond when the Lord calls? Like Mary, we can ask honest questions when we have them.

At times we may be tempted to imagine Mary at the Annunciation in far too simplistic a manner: one celestial pronouncement, one moment of human assent. Or we might assume that Mary was purely submissive rather than collaborative. Either of these interpretations vastly oversimplifies the exchange. When Mary said, "Let it be with me according to your word," she was saying yes not just to one request, but to a lifetime of collaboration with the Holy Spirit, and therefore the Trinity. She would offer her assent over and over throughout the mystery of her earthly life: on learning her heart would be pierced, on the flight into Egypt, on finding Jesus in the Temple, at the wedding feast at Cana, at the foot of the Cross, on the morning of Resurrection, and even at that ultimate infilling of the Holy Spirit, Pentecost—and a thousand times more throughout many ordinary days. We should be strengthened by this, encouraged to offer our own ongoing assent to the Holy Spirit, day by day inviting him to stir in us anew, and trusting that Mary, an expert in this sacred maneuver, will aid us in yielding to the Spirit.

"[Mary's] obedience," writes von Speyer, "is the prototype of every future instance of Christian obedience, which draws its whole meaning from the life of prayer and perception of God's will."[33] Which is to say, every time we say yes to God, Mary is there. Every time we declare our desire to follow the will of the Lord, Mary's yes is there in the midst of it, leading the way. And in those moments when we're not sure what to do, we can have confidence that she is there interceding, just as she did at the wedding feast at Cana, bringing our needs to the Lord and then encouraging us to "Do whatever he tells you" (John 2:5). We can lean on her patience as we work through the process of discernment; she knows all about waiting for God's word to be fulfilled.

As Von Speyer points out:

This Marian grace overflows to all Christians; if they have really said Yes, God assumes authority for the direction of their further life. . . . Even as incarnate Word, God does not want to grow in [Mary] in such a way that he uses her for a time and then drops her when he has achieved his purposes. . . . When he allows her to give him everything constantly in her human fashion, he also gives her everything in his divine, eternal fashion. The Mother is not separated from the fruit that she brings forth. . . . Rather it is part of her fruit that she becomes Mother of all Christians. Her own fruitfulness is the fruit of her assent.[34]

Mary's yes was not a single moment of blind submission, but a ready response to an invitation to co-create with the Holy Spirit—and it would course through her entire life. It would become a powerful river flowing into the very heart of heaven—a river we can jump into, a river to carry us, joining every yes of our lives with hers.

COLLABORATING WITH A CREATIVE GOD

If you're reading these pages, you have probably already given your assent to the Lord. You've probably already experienced annunciation moments, when the Holy Spirit came and you gave your assent to collaborate in some new work for the Lord. No doubt it is the Holy Spirit who does the heavy lifting in these collaborations, but nonetheless you have made yourself ready and said yes to the Lord.

Every subsequent decision you make is tied to that initial assent. Every choice is just a further unfolding of that moment, just as it was for Mary. And as we have seen, her yes wasn't only an act of assent, but a choice to enter into a co-creative relationship. God has not come to dictate our lives to us. That would make us robots and our freedom meaningless. He wants us to own and cultivate this great attribute of collaboration that he has shared with us, we who are created in his image and likeness. What an extraordinary honor he bestows on us—on you and me. Mary, who embraced this invitation so perfectly, so purely, is an invaluable guide to a deeper understanding of what this collaborative and co-creative relationship means for each of us.

At this point, you might be thinking, *But surely, we're making too much of this notion of collaboration or co-creation. Surely, it's an insult to God to suggest we would be capable of this. Surely, I must decrease and he must increase.*

Let's go back to the beginning. The Book of Genesis makes it very plain indeed.

Then God said, "Let us make humankind in our image, according to our likeness; and let them have dominion over the fish of the sea, and over the birds of the air, and over the cattle, and over all the wild animals of the earth, and over every creeping thing that creeps upon the earth."

> So God created humankind in his image,
>   in the image of God he created them;
>   male and female he created them. (Genesis 1:26-27)

We've heard a million sermons on this passage—that we have been created in God's image and likeness. But do we dwell enough on what attributes this then assigns to our own persons?

Reflecting on the moment of humanity's creation, Fr. John Wickham reminds us that:

At the moment when these marvelous words are being spoken ["in his image and likeness he created them"] *God is acting as Creator*, and he is calling us into an interpersonal relationship with himself. *It follows that we are meant to be co-creators with him.* That is what his image and likeness within us means. The rocks, the plants, the other animals do not have this *imago Dei.* Only humans do. . . . Every single human person bears this image of co-creative love at heart. Each one is uniquely valuable in this wondrous creation.[35]

How magnificent! How much the Lord must value us, our freedom, and our creativity. Humanity's creative collaboration with God calls to mind, for example, many of the great religious movements of the Church—the witness of the desert Fathers who pursued holiness in the wilderness, the Benedictines, the Franciscans, Missionaries of Charity, Sisters of Life, Jesuits, Dominicans, and Companions of Christ, and on and on and on. All brought to fruition through the holiest of collaborations—and look at the fruit they have wrought over the millennia.

Von Speyer builds on this notion when she writes,

[Mary] resolves to let God alone work; and yet, precisely by virtue of this resolution, she becomes cooperative. For cooperation with the action of grace is always the fruit of renunciation. Every renunciation in love is fruitful because it makes room for consent to God, and God waits only for a person's consent to show him what a man is capable of doing with God's help.[36]

God makes us capable of great creative feats of virtue, beauty, holiness, service, and sacrifice. When I find myself straining to make a *graced* decision—one that reflects my desire to collaborate with God—it can help to consider my approach. Instead of asking, "What does God want me to do?" I can reframe the question this way: "Lord, what shall we co-create together? How shall we bring more of you into this present circumstance?"

Mary did not abandon her freedom; she offered it in her body and blood shared with an infant, and the result of that co-creation was nothing less than the Savior of the world—the precious Body and Blood we celebrate and consume at every Mass. We can trust that our collaborations with the Holy Spirit will also be made more fruitful and effective according to the call of God in our own life.

Becoming Who You Are

I'll be honest: sometimes I fear collaboration with God Almighty, Creator of the Universe, King of Kings, and Lord of Lords. Mary's life was beautiful but far from easy. If I join in co-creating with the Lord, will it mean the annihilation of my desires, my hopes? Will a sword piece my heart, too? Am I going to have to sacrifice all of myself for what God wants?

Well, yes—and no.

It is helpful to consider the Blessed Sacrament: Mary's assent made this gift a reality and ties her life forever to the Eucharist. Just as the bread and wine of the Holy Mass are not destroyed at the moment of consecration but *transformed* into the Precious Body and Blood of Christ, so I am not destroyed, but *transformed* when collaborating and cooperating with the Holy Spirit—trans-formed into the person God made me to be.[37] There can be no greater freedom than to be who I am.

Fr. Wilfrid Stinissen is very helpful here, reminding us that the love that is the Holy Spirit *makes you who you are.* And when you become an instrument of the Spirit and allow him to work in you, you in your turn help others to become real persons. . . . *I become more who I am, and you become more who you are*, which enables us to have deep, personal relationships.[38]

Did you catch that? Collaborating with the Holy Spirit makes me more myself. Far from quashing me, collaboration with the Holy Spirit makes it possible for me to use my charisms, my spiritual gifts, and to become who I am meant to be. There is no greater fulfillment, no purer joy than when we are active in our charisms. And that helps others to become who they are meant to be. The fruitfulness expands.

This is precisely what is unfolding at the Annunciation: Mary is becoming exactly who she is meant to be, who she has been created to be, the mother of God. This must have brought her the greatest joy and fulfillment she could have known. Ultimately that is the work of the Holy Spirit: to help us to know the deepest desires of our heart, given to us by the Father, and to help us become who we are meant to be in his kingdom.

Fr. Stinissen writes: "The goal of the Incarnation, the Cross, and the Resurrection is Pentecost. If God has become man, if he has suffered and died for us and risen from the dead, it is in order finally to fill us with the Holy Spirit."[39] That very same Holy Spirit who overshadowed the Blessed Mother is the same Holy Spirit who visits us in the sacraments and in our prayer, through God's word and through holy relationships. That same Holy Spirit, the great transformer, is not an optional person of the Trinity, he is necessary to your flourishing and what's more, he's already within you. If you receive the sacraments, if you are praying and spending time in God's word, you can be confident that the Holy Spirit is at work.

Let's return to the women from the beginning of this chapter for a moment—women struggling earnestly to make graced decisions about incredibly important things. It's unlikely an angel will appear to either of them to provide a miraculous way forward. The Lord loves us in our freedom too much to dictate such things to us. Yes, he does offer us concrete lists to guide our decisions: the Ten Commandments, for example, and the spiritual and corporal works of mercy. But we also work diligently with the Holy Spirit to discern the best path forward. We want to do as Mary did: to bring him what we have and allow him to touch us, to magnify us. We pray for clarity of heart to know the desires of our heart; we pray to be graced and to know who we are in the Lord.

If the young woman I described in my first story decided to marry her Christian boyfriend, the Lord would not remove his hand from her life. Regardless of her decision, God would not abandon her. And so she prayed and struggled and discerned, and as she did, the way forward became clear.

One day she was visiting with friends from her missionary days, two young men and a young woman. They all went to Mass together, and it was there, before the Blessed Sacrament, that she had a kind of annunciation moment. (How often the Lord speaks to us through the Real Presence.) While standing with her friends, all of them joining in the various refrains throughout the Mass, singing the Gloria and saying the Creed together, heaven invited her into deeper collaboration.

"I heard these male voices speaking with me, responding with me, and it struck me," she recalled. "How different it was to go to Mass with [my boyfriend] who did not join in the prayers. Then standing there with these men, our voices in unison, I realized how much I needed that." In that moment, she recognized who she was and what she was created for, and she leaned into this. You might say that she cooperated and collaborated with this moment of annunciation.

Our other friend, struggling in a troubled marriage, is still waiting to make a decision about staying or leaving, separation or even divorce. Or perhaps the Lord will provide a resolution she has not yet considered. She exhibits heroic patience as she pulls together the pieces of information she needs to make a decision about how to move forward in fruitfulness. She stands in the painful place of trusting the Lord to help her make not just a good decision, but a graced one—one that results in more life and not annihilation.

She meditates often on Mary's river of assent. With confidence, she invites Mary into this collaboration. As Von Speyer writes,

All forms of Christian fruitfulness are patterned on Mary. . . . Her perfections go out from her like rays and strike all the faithful regardless of age, gender, or state of life, to develop in them in the most diverse ways.[40]

And no doubt, Mary's patience and forbearance strengthen her in her own.

EMBRACING THE DIVINE MISSION WITH THE BLESSED MOTHER

Community is one of the greatest blessings given to us through the Holy Trinity and the Church. We never have to make the most important decisions of our lives in isolation. The whole communion of saints joins us, intercedes for us. First and foremost in this collaboration is the Blessed Mother.

As Von Speyer writes:

> [Jesus] needs co-workers, and he seeks them; but only a few listen to his call. So the Mother works with him by sharing the power of her assent with each person until his response becomes an actual Yes to the Son. She stretches all our efforts until they reach the Son, just as the Son stretches our efforts until they reach the Father. She does not wait to do this until someone calls her by name; she turns to the Son even prayers in which she is not mentioned. Thus the Mother and the Son work together.[41]

This is precisely what we are invited to do too, to co-create with the graces provided by heaven so that our lives become truly fruitful.

The last thing Scripture tells us about the earthly life of Mary is that she was in the Upper Room at Pentecost when the Holy Spirit descended on the disciples. As her life was covered beginning to end in a living collaboration with the Holy Spirit, ours can be, too. Let's pray often and always for the grace to collaborate and co-create with our Creator, guided by the Holy Spirit and in imitation of Mary in her life-giving assent at the Annunciation.

Pray

Blessed Mother, pray for us, that we may embrace the greatness of our creativity. That like you, we will collaborate with the divine mission to which we have been called and that the fruit of this collaboration will be nothing less than the Christing of the world. We ask this through Our Lord, Jesus Christ, your son, Amen.

Ponder

1. Ask the Holy Spirit to join you in your prayer time. Trust that when you ask him to come, he comes. Then, asking for the grace of a more deeply collaborative heart, one that wishes to co-create with the Holy Spirit, pray with the following verses, reading them over slowly several times. Pay attention to the words or phrases that really capture your attention and rest with them.

When the day of Pentecost had come, they were all together in one place. And suddenly from heaven there came a sound like the rush of a violent wind, and it filled the entire house where they were sitting. Divided tongues, as of fire, appeared among them, and a tongue rested on each of them. All of them were filled with the Holy Spirit and began to speak in other languages, as the Spirit gave them ability. (Acts 2:1-4)

2. Try to place yourself in the room at Pentecost. Try to imagine the tongues of fire coming to rest on you. What happens? How does this affect you? Rest in that moment a while. What thoughts or feelings come into your heart in this time?

3. Far from quashing me, collaboration with the Holy Spirit makes it possible for me to use my charisms, my spiritual gifts, and to become who I am meant to be. There is no greater fulfillment, no purer joy than when we are active in our charisms. And that helps others to become who they are meant to be. Think of one situation in your life today, and ask the Lord, "What shall we co-create together? How shall we bring more of you into this present circumstance?" Journal or share his response.

4. When Mary said, "Be it done unto me," she was saying "yes" not just to one request, but to a lifetime of collaboration with the Holy Spirit. Have you experienced this in your own life? Has it been more challenging to say "yes" at some times than at other times?

ABOUT THE AUTHOR

Elizabeth (Liz) Kelly is popular speaker and retreat leader and the award-winning author or co-author of thirteen books.

NOTES

[1] Thomas Merton, *Emblems of a Season of Fury* (Norfolk, CT: New Directions, 1963), 66.

[2] "Sophia: Wisdom of God," Center for Action and Contemplation, https://cac .org/daily-meditations/sophia-wisdom-of-god-2017-11-07/.

[3] The accounts of Matthew and Mark are similar (Matthew 26:6-13; Mark 14:3- 9), but John's is rather different (John 12:1-8). In John, the woman is identified as Mary, sister of Martha and Lazarus, and the anointing takes place six days before Passover rather than two. She anoints his feet rather than his head, and wipes them with her hair. All three Gospels note that the anointing took place in Bethany, but Matthew and Mark identify the home as that of Simon the Leper.

Luke recounts an episode that has some similarities but may refer to a different event: earlier in Jesus' ministry, a sinful woman of the city weeps on Jesus' feet and anoints them, wiping them with her hair (Luke 7:37-50). Luke identifies the host as Simon, a Pharisee.

[4] This is one possible explanation for why the woman is anonymous in Matthew and Mark, but named in the Gospel of John, written decades later when any danger of prosecution would have passed.

[5] Mark does not identify the guests who were enraged, but Matthew 26:8 tells us that they were Jesus' disciples. John 12:4-6 records that it was specifically Judas who criticized her.

[6] Watchman Nee, "Why This Waste?," https://godchaserslibrary.files.wordpress .com/2017/11/watchman-nee-why-this-waste-nee.pdf, 6.

[7] See Nee, "Why This Waste?," 23.

[8] See Mark 1:13, 31; Luke 8:3. The verb for "minister to" or "serve" in these verses, *diakoneō*, is the origin of our words "deacon" and "diaconate." It is the same verb Jesus uses in summing up the purpose of his own coming: "The Son of Man came not to be served, but to serve" (Mark 10:45).

[9] The same word is used in the expression "give alms" in Tobit 12:8; "good works" in Matthew 5:16.

[10] The command "Do this in memory of me" (see Luke 22:19; 1 Corinthians 11:24) does not occur in Mark; however, the ritual language used in his Last Supper account indicates that he was familiar with the early Christian liturgy that retold and re-presented Jesus' self-gift on the cross.

[11] "Prayer of St. Ephraim," Jeff and Emily Cavins, May 1, 2008, https://www .jeffcavins.com/2008-5-1-let-the-fountain-quench-your-thirst-html/.

[12] Alice Camille, "Why Didn't the Jews and Samaritans Get Along?," *U.S. Catholic*, May 14, 2020, https://uscatholic.org/articles/202005/why-didnt-the-jews -and-samaritans-get-along/

[13]   Pope John Paul II, *Mulieris Dignitatem*, 31, https://www.vatican.va/content/john-paul-ii/en/apost_letters/1988/documents/hf_jp-ii_apl_19880815_mulieris-dignitatem.html.

[14]   Archbishop Allen H. Vigneron, "The Power of the Word of God," January 24, 2021, cf. Pope Francis, *Aperuit Illis*, 8, https://www.unleashthegospel.org/pastoral-notes/the-power-of-the-word-of-god/.

[15]   Duncan Robertson, *Lectio Divina: The Medieval Experience of Reading* (Trappist, KY: Cistercian Publications, 2011), xvii.

[16]   See Timothy Gray, *Praying Scripture for a Change: An Introduction to Lectio Divina* (West Chester, PA: Ascension Press, 2008).

[17]   Pope Paul VI, *Evangelii Nuntiandi*, December 8, 1975, 24, https://www.vatican.va/content/paul-vi/en/apost_exhortations/documents/hf_p-vi_exh_19751208_evangelii-nuntiandi.html.

[18]   Pope Benedict XVI, Angelus, February 24, 2008, https://www.vatican.va/content/benedict-xvi/en/angelus/2008/documents/hf_ben-xvi_ang_20080224.html.

[19]   Pope Benedict XVI, Homily, April 24, 2005, https://www.vatican.va/content/benedict-xvi/en/homilies/2005/documents/hf_ben-xvi_hom_20050424_inizio-pontificato.html.

[20]   "Divine Mercy 101: What Is Divine Mercy?," *The Divine Mercy,* November 22, 2021, https://www.thedivinemercy.org/articles/divine-mercy-101-what-divine-mercy.

[21]   For this insight, I am deeply indebted to Kelly Walhquist, *Created to Relate: God's Design for Peace and Joy* (Cincinnati, OH: Franciscan Media, 2015).

[22]   See Numbers 20:1-13; Deuteronomy 32:51-52

[23]   Personal correspondence, 2012.

[24]   Rhonda Garelick, "What We Lose When We Loosen Dress Code," *The New York Times*, September 22, 2023, https://www.nytimes.com/2023/09/22/style/senate-dress-code-politics.html.

[25]   Ibid.

[26]   Jane Ridley, "More People Die Taking Selfies Than in Shark Attacks," *New York Post*, February 14, 2020, https://nypost.com/2020/02/14/more-people-die-taking-selfies-than-in-shark-attacks-survey/.

[27]   This is the numbering in the NABRE. For those using the RSV2CE, it is 15:1.

[28]   Elizabeth Hale, "Our Gold Standard," *The Irish Rover,* September 9, 2023, https://irishrover.net/2023/09/our-golden-standard.

[29] Swiss medical doctor, Adrienne von Speyr (1902–1967) was a convert to Catholicism, a mystic, and a writer who authored more than sixty volumes on spirituality and theology. *Handmaid of the Lord* is considered one of her most important contributions to the wisdom of the Church. She was a close collaborator with the Swiss theologian Hans Urs von Balthasar, who was her confessor for twenty-seven years. Together they founded the Community of St. John.

[30] Adrienne von Speyr, *Handmaid of the Lord* (Ignatius Press: San Francisco, 1985), 20, emphasis mine.

[31] See Caryll Houselander, *Essential Writings*, ed. Wendy M. Wright (Maryknoll, NY: Orbis Books, 2005), 11.

[32] *The Annunciation* by Simone Martini, Fra Angelico, and Sandro Botticelli portray Mary as steeped in Scripture when the angel appears, to name just three.

[33] Von Speyr, *Handmaid of the Lord*, 33.

[34] Von Speyr, *Handmaid of the Lord*, 43.

[35] John Wickham, SJ, *The Common Faith* (Montreal: Ignatian Centre Publications, 1990), 36-37, emphasis mine.

[36] Von Speyr, *Handmaid of the Lord*, 13.

[37] See Wilfrid Stinissen, OCD, *Bread That Is Broken*, trans. Sr. Clare Marie, OCD (San Francisco: Ignatius Press, 2020), 56-57:

The transformation of bread and wine in the Eucharist teaches us that transformation is something fundamental in our lives. Everything can be transformed. It is enough to "offer" it, to lay it on the paten. The priest's gesture of sacrifice shows that the object must be lifted up and offered to God for transformation. Nothing may only lie on the earth. It must be set into a new context where it receives a new meaning. Everything that we offer in the Eucharist together with the bread and the wine—our joy, our sorrow, even our sins—becomes transformed. Everything that was a minus becomes a plus. Everything becomes grace. . . .
    [God] is the great transformer. But he transforms only what we give him. Bread that is not presented remains ordinary bread. Much in our life remains as it was, much stagnates, because it is not offered up.

[38] Wilfrid Stinissen, OCD, *The Holy Spirit, Fire of Divine Love*, trans. Sr. Clare Marie, OCD (San Francisco: Ignatius Press, 2017), 35, emphasis mine.

[39] Wilfrid Stinissen, *The Holy Spirit, Fire of Divine Love*, 19.

[40] Von Speyer, *Handmaid of the Lord*, 194.

[41] Von Speyer, *Handmaid of the Lord*, 191.

About the Authors

Kelly Wahlquist is the founder of the national women's ministry WINE: Women In the New Evangelization and the director for the Archbishop Flynn Catechetical Institute at The Saint Paul Seminary in the Archdiocese of Saint Paul and Minneapolis. She is also a contributing writer for Catholicmom.com, the author of *Created to Relate: God's Design for Peace & Joy*, and the editor of *Walk in Her Sandals: Experiencing the Passion of Christ through the Eyes of Women* and *Gaze Upon Jesus: Experiencing Christ's Childhood through the Eyes of Women*, which are innovative collaborative works that allow women to enter into their relationship with Jesus in the way in which they were created to—as women. Find out more at KellyWahlquist.com.

Alyssa Bormes is an educator, author, speaker, writer, and emcee. She teaches Scripture at Chesterton Academy in Hopkins, MN to ninth and tenth graders and is an instructor at the Archbishop Flynn Catechetical Institute. She wrote the foreword to and orchestrated the publication of *The Mother of Jesus is Wonderfully Real*, by Father Paul Murray, OP, which was endorsed by Bishop Robert Barron. She is the author of *The Catechism of Hockey*, an editor for *Called by Name: 365 Daily Devotions for Catholic Women*, a contributor for *Gaze on Jesus: Experiencing Christ's Childhood through the Eyes of Women*, wrote for the foreword to *Contraception and Persecution*, by Charles E. Rice, is a blog writer for WINE: Women in the New Evangelization, and has appeared in other Catholic publications. Her talk, The Hope and Healing of Humanae Vitae, has been praised and can be found on CatholicVineyard.com. In 2023, she spoke with Minnesota Concerned Citizens for Life (MCCL) at the March for Life. For seven-and-a-half years, she was the host of Catholic Kaleidoscope on Radio Maria US. Alyssa has spoken throughout the country on a variety of topics, and she is an accomplished emcee.

Dr. Mary Healy is professor of Scripture at Sacred Heart Major Seminary in Detroit and a bestselling author and international speaker. She is a general editor of the *Catholic Commentary on Sacred Scripture* and author of two of its volumes, *The Gospel of Mark* and *Hebrews*. Her other books include *The Spiritual Gifts Handbook* and *Healing*. Dr. Healy is one of the first three women ever to serve on the Pontifical Biblical Commission, and is a consultor to the Dicastery for Divine Worship and the Discipline of the Sacraments. Her website is drmaryhealy.com.

Elizabeth (Liz) Kelly is popular speaker and retreat leader and the award-winning author or co-author of thirteen books, including *A Place Called Golgotha: Meditations on the Last Words of Christ*, *Love Like a Saint: Cultivating Virtue with Holy Women*, and *Jesus Approaches, What Contemporary Women Can Learn about Healing, Freedom & Joy from the Women of the New Testament*. She focuses on the Ignatian exercises and leads retreats with a particular focus on helping women to flourish in their faith. Kelly's written works frequently appear in the Magnificat's Lenten and Advent Companions, as well as the *Catholic Spirit*, *Blessed is She*, and other Catholic venues. Kelly holds advanced degrees in Creating Writing and Catholic Studies and received her certification as a spiritual director in 2015. From 2008 to 2022, she served as the managing editor of Logos: A Journal of Catholic Thought and Culture at the Center for Catholic Studies in St. Paul, Minnesota, where she also taught in the Catholic Studies program at the University of St. Thomas. Kelly has appeared on Relevant Radio, Catholic Answers, Radio Maria, Public Radio, Boston Catholic Television, EWTN, and Salt and Light Television. Visit her website at LizK.org or follow her on Instagram at LizKToday.

Melissa Overmyer is the founder of Something Greater Ministries, which provides opportunities for people to encounter God through prayer; Scripture study; community; and the teachings, traditions, and spirituality of the Catholic Church. She has been a Scripture study teacher for more than thirty years, and founded the Georgetown Women's Bible Study, an interdenominational women's scripture study, twenty-seven years ago. Melissa is the author of *Metamorphosis of a Soul*, *Born to Soar*, *Unleashing God's Word in Your Life*, and *From Worry to Wonder, A Catholic Guide to Finding Peace Through Scripture*. She loves her husband, family, and leading pilgrimages to the Holy Land. Find her at melissaovermyer.com.

Teresa Tomeo is the author of over ten books, syndicated Catholic talk show host, and motivational speaker with over thirty years of experience in TV, radio, and newspaper. She hosts Catholic Connection on Ave Maria Radio and the EWTN Global Catholic Radio Network and owns T's Italy, a travel consultation company specializing in all things Italy. She and her husband, Deacon Dominick Pastore, travel the world giving marriage and diaconate couples retreats. You can find her at TravelItalyExpert.com and TeresaTomeo.com.

The Word Among Us publishes a monthly devotional magazine, books, Bible studies, and pamphlets that help Catholics grow in their faith.

To learn more about who we are and what we publish, visit www.wau.org. There you will find a variety of Catholic resources that will help you grow in your faith.

Your review makes a difference! If you enjoyed this book, please consider sharing your review on Amazon using the QR code below.

Embrace His Word
Listen to God . . .

www.wau.org

Made in United States
Troutdale, OR
01/29/2024

17274863R00077